John Gerhard's Manual of Comfort

Especially for the Severely Ill

Translated, Abridged, and Adapted by John M. Drickamer

From the German Version of Carl Julius Boettcher

Illustrated by James B. Romnes

Revised Edition

John Gerhard's Manual of Comfort, as translated, abridged, and adapted by John M. Drickamer, from the German Version of Carl Julius Boettcher.

Text Copyright © 1995, 1996, 1997, 2020 John M. Drickamer
Illustrations Copyright © 1995, 1996, 1997, 2020 James B. Romnes

All rights reserved. No part of this book may be reproduced or transmitted in any form or by any means, electronic or mechanical, including photocopying, recording or by any information storage and retrieval system without prior written permission from the author and/or the artist, except for the inclusion of brief quotations in a review, or as allowed below.

Reprint Permission for Christian Organizations: Any portion of this book may be reprinted in bulletins, newsletters, pamphlets, brochures, etc. prepared for free distribution in your church or Christian organization on the condition that the following copyright notice is included: "Reprinted from the "Revised Edition" of *John Gerhard's Manual of Comfort,* Copyright © 1997 John M. Drickamer and James B. Romnes."

All illustrations contained in this book, © 1995, 1996, 1997, were produced for *Christian News* by James B. Romnes, used with permission.

The complete original text, by John M. Drickamer, and illustrations, by James B. Romnes, of *John Gerhard's Manual of Comfort* were printed in the Monday, December 2, 1996, issue of *Christian News,* Vol. 34, No. 45.

Unless otherwise indicated, Scripture is taken from *The Authorized King James Version* of the Holy Bible.

The layout, typesetting, and initial printing of this "Revised Edition" in book form was donated to *Christian News* by "fellow servants" of our Lord and Savior, Christ Jesus.

These "fellow servants" hope and pray that "seed projects," such as this one, will develop their own broad support of individuals, who will not only pay for their own copy of this book to read and share with others, but also make tax-deductible donations to *Christian News* to provide for the free distribution of this book to students, seminarians, chaplains, deaconness, etc., as many *Christian News* subscribers do in sharing their weekly issue with others and in making tax-deductible donations to *Christian News* to enable the free mailing of their weekly publication to many others.

Library of Congress Card
Lutheran News, Inc.
684 Luther Lane
New Haven, MO 63068
Published 2012
Printed in the United States of America,
Lightning Source, Inc.
LaVergne, TN, USA 37086
ISBN 978-0-9864232-9-1

Introduction

Boettcher rightly calls this work a gem. A major value of the book is that Gerhard asks the right questions. If more people asked these questions today, the work of the faithful pastor would be much more direct, and churches where God's Word is purely preached would be full.

The questions Gerhard puts into the mouth of the afflicted person may sound strange. But they are the real questions of sufferers, even if most people today would phrase them differently. People have these concerns when facing death. More than anything else, death can still confront modern man with spiritual need. Who but God can help in the face of disease, disaster, and death?

The book has been considerably abridged, altered, and adapted. Many statements have been completely rephrased. I have been much freer with the text than would be proper if the purpose were scholarly research in Gerhard's thought. The book still presents the original, Biblical, evangelical comfort. But I have taken liberties with the wording to provide a helpful book that will hopefully not be misunderstood in the confusing theological climate of modern America.

Any good content in the book can be traced to Scripture. Any good phrasing may be ascribed to Gerhard and Boettcher. Any faults should be laid at my door.

No attempt has been made to trace the references to the writings of theologians. Gerhard mentions ancient and medieval Christian writers such as Augustine of Hippo and Bernard of Clairvaux. The interested reader could look them up in a dictionary of Christian history. There are also references to the Apocrypha, ancient Jewish writings in Greek from before the time of the New Testament. Luther noted that these are useful books but are by no means on the same level as the Bible. The interested reader can find further information in his church library or with his pastor's help.

Boettcher's title page reads: **Enchiridion consolatorium: oder Troestliches Handbuechlein Johann Gerhard's wider** den Tod und die Anfechtungen beim Todeskampfe. Aus dem Lateinischen uebersetzt von Carl Julius Boettcher, Ev. Luth. Pastor. Leipzig: Verlag von Justus Naumann, 1877. That is: **Handbook of Comforts: Or Comforting Little Handbook of John Gerhard Against Death and the Temptations in the Struggle of Death.** Translated from the Latin by Carl Julius Boettcher, Evangelical Lutheran Pastor. Leipzig: Publishing House of Justus Naumann, 1877. In a footnote in the foreword he gives the complete title as: **Handbuechlein kraeftigen Trostes, welchen man dem Tode und den Anfechtungen in der Todesnoth kann entgegensetzen.** That is: **Little Handbook of Powerful Comfort Which One Can Set Against Death and the Temptations in the Emergency of Death.** I have chosen the title Manual of Comfort. "Manual" is based on the Latin word for "hand," and so corresponds exactly to the German **Handbuch** and the Greek enchiridion.

Gerhard uses the word **Troester,** "comforter," for the pastor or anyone who brings God's Word to help the afflicted person. That is the word Luther used for the Holy Spirit, the Comforter. The title shows that those who correctly comfort and encourage others spiritually with God's Word are sharing with them the means by which the Holy Spirit performs His blessed work. To God alone belongs all glory for spiritual benefit. But it is a wonder that we poor vessels are privileged to have a role in this work. That should not make us proud. It should make us humble — but glad.

Angels could speak the Word better than you or I, but they have not experienced the afflictions. Angels are wiser and stronger than we. We who comfort our fellow sufferers/fellow believers, need the very same comfort which we share with them. If the teacher learns by teaching, the comforter is comforted by comforting.

God bless this work to His glory, for the salvation of precious souls for whom Christ shed His blood on the altar of the cross.

John M. Drickamer

Boettcher's Foreword (Abridged)

The Manual of Comfort is a gem of edifying Lutheran literature. It came into being in 1611 and was written in Latin. Its author, the great Lutheran dogmatician, John Gerhard, was at that time, though very young, the Superintendent at Heldburg in the Meining area. The work which establishes his fame, the dogmatics known as the 'Loci theologici,' was begun during his years at Heldburg. He was always concerned to apply doctrine to life. This manual of comfort against death grew alongside the learned 'Loci.' The 'Loci' are like the great garden of nature in which all kinds of useful vegetation thrive. This little manual may be compared to a herb garden in which one who understands healing has planted the choicest medicinal herbs.

The great theologian arranged the medicine garden at first for himself. It was a difficult time for him. On January 10 of the year named, his first and, until then, only son died. In May the young mother followed the child. While they fought against death, John Gerhard also collapsed with broken health. But his inner man was not broken. That was accomplished by the medicinal herbs which he knew from God's Word. He planted them together in a medical garden to strengthen his soul a few weeks before his wife was called home. He composed it in Latin, but we will hardly be mistaken if we assume that he presented now the one, now the other herb to the departing soul that was so precious to him, as it was necessary for her. This little book has been experienced and proven by the author himself as few others have been.

This little book will never leave the pastor in the lurch in facing souls that need comfort. Those who care for the sick will find in it precious answers for the questions of doubt with which the soul can be made anxious in the final struggle. Even the afflicted soul, if it has used the book, can draw from it the needed herb for itself.

The little book was translated into German shortly after it was published. But the various translations did not seem to satisfy the author. So he published his own translation in 1626. I have searched for Gerhard's translation, but I have never found anything of it. That can be explained. Such small writings have seldom been included in the scholarly libraries. They have commonly been worn out in the homes.

As excellently as the dear Gerhard understood how to write Latin, so poor was his ability with German. The learned language adhered to him so that he wrote German in a very cumbersome style. I suspect that Gerhard's translation, if anyone would discover it, would not differ substantially in style from that of his brother-in-law, Schroeter, the only one that I could find, which is almost completely unusable by a sick person in our day. In all modesty I am letting my translation be issued because the little book must not be lost to the German Lutheran church and its pastors.

The Lord accompany it with His blessing!

Sachsenburg bei Frankenberg in Saxony,
February 1, 1877.

Carl Julius Boettcher
Evangelical Lutheran Pastor

Table of Contents

1. Facing Death 1
2. The Sting of Death 2
3. Anxiety about Sins 3
4. My Many Sins 5
5. Do I Benefit from Christ's Death? 7
6. Is My Faith Genuine? 9
7. Repentant Sorrow 11
8. Terror of Conscience 13
9. Temptation to Despair 15
10. Temptation to Blasphemy 17
11. Is the Gospel for Everyone? 18
12. Does God Reject Anyone Arbitrarily? 20
13. Can Christ's Merit Be Mine? 23
14. Is the Word of Absolution True? 25
15. The Baptismal Covenant 28
16. The Assurance of Grace 30
17. Worthy Reception of the Lord's Supper 32
18. My Faith Is Weak 34
19. Faith and Feeling 36
20. I Cannot Believe 38
21. I Do So Few Good Works 39
22. What Merit Do I Have? 41
23. The Law Accuses Me 42
24. My Conscience Accuses Me 44
25. My Repentance Comes Too Late 46
26. Is God Gracious? 47
27. I Am Not Ready to Die 50
28. Does the Holy Spirit Dwell in Me? 52
29. Will I Persevere in the Faith? 55
30. The Devil's Deceit and Power 57
31. Will I Fall Away? 59

32. Am I Written in the Book of Life? 61
33. Fear of Death 63
34. The Wages of Sin 65
35. The Pains of Death 68
36. An Early Death 70
37. I Could Do More for God's Kingdom 71
38. Have I Shortened My Own Life? 73
39. Love for Life 74
40. Separation from Spouse, Children, and Family 76
41. Deafness Just Before Death 78
42. Why Do the Redeemed Still Die? 80
43. Fear of the Dust 81
44. The Resurrection Is Contrary to Reason 84
45. Purgatory 86
46. The Strictness of the Last Judgment 88

A Prayer in Severe Illness .... Back Cover

1. Facing Death

The afflicted person says: My illness could be terminal. I know I am mortal anyway. But this life still seems sweet. This world still seems beautiful. The only life I know is this life in this body.

The comforter says: God created you, not for this poor, short life, but for everlasting life. God created Adam and Eve, our first parents, to live forever.

You were redeemed by Christ not for this hard life but for that blessed life waiting for you in heaven. "This is a faithful saying, and worthy of all acceptation, that Christ Jesus came into the world to save sinners" (1 Tim. 1:15).

Through the Gospel the Holy Spirit has called you into Christ's kingdom, not to be happy for a little while on earth, but to move one day from the kingdom of grace to the kingdom of glory, from the church militant to the church triumphant, from the vale of tears to the land of joy.

"If in this life only we have hope in Christ, we are of all men most miserable" (1 Cor. 15:19). If you are soon to be led through the door of death into the life for which the Father created you, the Son redeemed you, and the Holy Spirit called you, do not reject the gracious will of God toward you (Luke 7:30). If God is calling you, follow with all joy!

2. The Sting of Death

The afflicted person says: The thought of dying terrifies me. It makes me anxious and afraid. Sin, the sting of death (1 Cor. 15:56), threatens me with God's anger against my sins. "For the wages of sin is death" (Rom. 6:23). It is because of sin that I am mortal like everyone else (Rom. 5:18).

The comforter says: If your sins terrify your heart, look to Christ Who died for you on the altar of the cross so that you do not have to die everlasting death. Turn your eyes away from the outward form of death and turn them to Christ. He came "that through death He might destroy him that had the power of death, that is, the devil; and deliver them who through fear of death were all their lifetime subject to bondage" (Heb. 2:14-15).

Christ has put our death to death and ended the threat of hell that we had deserved (Hos. 13:14). "I am the resurrection, and the life: he that believeth in Me, though he were dead, yet shall he live: And whosoever liveth and believeth in Me shall never die" (John 11:25-26).

As we have become mortal in Adam, because of inherited sin and by committing sins; we will be made alive in Christ (1 Cor. 15:22), the Lord of life, the Conqueror of death. The Lord Himself confirmed that: "Verily, verily, I say unto you, He that heareth My Word, and believeth on Him that sent Me, hath everlasting life, and shall not come into condemnation; but is passed from death unto life" (John 5:24). "Verily, verily, I say unto you, If a man keep My saying, he shall never see death" (John 8:51).

Believe in Christ, for He is the truth (John 14:6). Believe Him, for He has promised it. Believe Him, for He has sworn it. "Heaven and earth shall pass away: But My words shall not pass away" (Luke 21:33).

3. Anxiety about Sin

The afflicted person says: I remember many sins I have committed. I was conceived and born in sin, and all my life I have committed many various sins. How can I hope that God will be gracious to me since I have offended Him so many times? How can I have any comfort in the face of death since I deserve to die for my sins and all who die without God's grace go to hell?

The comforter says: Look to Christ crucified, Who paid the ransom for you. He shed His precious blood for your sins. "The blood of Jesus Christ His Son cleanseth us from all sin" (1 John 1:7). "And He is the propitiation for our sins: and not for our's only, but also for the sins of the whole world" (1 John 2:2). "The Son of Man came... to give His life a ransom for many" (Matt. 20:28). So that no doubt arises in your heart, the angel brought from heaven the sweet, comforting name "Jesus" and gave it to our Mediator "before He was conceived. in the womb" (Luke 2:21). "Jesus" means nothing other than "Savior." Christ was given this name "for He shall save His people from their sins" (Matt. 1:21).

He is "the Lamb of God, Which taketh away the sin of the world" (John 1:29). Jesus Christ "came into the world to save sinners" (I Tim. 1:15). The High Priest of the New Testament "hath given Himself for us an offering and a sacrifice to God for a sweet smelling savour" (Eph. 5:2). Christ shed His own blood "for many for the remission of sins" (Matt. 26:28). He Himself "bore our sins in His own body on the tree" (1 Pet. 2:24). He was "wounded for our transgressions, He was bruised for our iniquities" (Is. 53:5).

The Lord has cast all our sin on Him. God "hath made Him to be sin [a sin offering] for us, Who knew no sin" (2 Cor. 5:21). He laid the punishment for our sins on Himself. God made Jesus the sacrificial Lamb for our sins.

Christ did not resist the will of His Father but did it willingly (Ps. 40:8). He "gave Himself for our sins" (Gal. 1:4). He loved us and gave Himself for us (Gal. 2:20). Love moved

Him. As great as the pain in His suffering was, His love toward us was greater. With this love He would have endured even more if the price He paid for our redemption had not been enough.

We need not doubt that His ransom was sufficient; for with Him is plenteous redemption (Ps. 130:7). Not only one drop but a whole stream of blood flowed from His wounds. At the last He cried out that everything had been accomplished (John 19:30). He brought about a complete and total cleansing of our sins through Himself (Heb. 1:3). "For by one offering He hath perfected for ever them that are sanctified" (Heb. 10:14). He "washed us from our sins in His own blood" (Rev. 1:5). So believe these clear words of the Holy Spirit and be certain and sure that through Christ's suffering and death a sufficient satisfaction was paid for your sins, too.

> "...Christ Jesus came into the world to save sinners. I am the worst of them..."
> I Timothy 1:15

4. My Many Sins

The afflicted person says: Maybe Christ took away only original sin, and I have to pay for my sinful thoughts, words, and deeds, or burn in hell forever. I know my inherited guilt has been washed away by Christ, but I am worried about all the sins I have committed all my life. They richly deserve damnation. Christ is the counterpart of Adam (Rom. 5:18). Maybe Christ's work extends only as far as Adam's sin. Another's guilt can be paid for by another, but one must pay for one's own guilt.

The comforter says: "The blood of Jesus Christ His Son cleanseth us from all sin" (1 John 1:7), not only what you inherited from Adam, but also all you have committed. "God hath set forth [Christ] to be a propitiation through faith in His blood" (Rom. 3:25). We may go to Him in true faith, ask for forgiveness, and know God's grace whenever the heavy burden of sin weighs us down. We may "come boldly unto the throne of grace, that we may obtain mercy, and find grace to help in time of need" (Heb. 4:16).

What kind of redemption and reconciliation would that be if Christ had paid for one type of sin and we had to pay for all others, for more and heavier sins? Christ's redemption is no such piecemeal, imperfect, halfway redemption. He has "offered one sacrifice for sins for ever" (Heb. 10:12). "By one offering He hath perfected for ever them that are sanctified" (Heb. 10:14). "And if any man sin, we have an Advocate with the Father, Jesus Christ the righteous: And He is the propitiation for our sins: and not for our's only, but also for the sins of the whole world" (1 John 2:1-2).

When we fall into sins through weakness of our flesh, we may in true repentance find a refuge in Christ. He intercedes for us on the basis of His merit. Christ's prayer for us is effective because He has made a complete and totally satisfactory payment for our sins.

The mighty arm of God's strict judgment does not extend over us as we have deserved because Christ has paid the ransom price for us and covered our sins with the blanket of His mercy. It must always remain firmly established that through His death Christ has offered the only true sacrifice for us and has removed, destroyed, and extinguished all our guilt. In Him and through Him we have the forgiveness of sins, not only of original sin but also of all the others we have added.

Hold it firmly in your heart that Christ gave Himself for us that He might redeem us from all iniquity (Titus 2:14). He Who paid for our sins is infinite; how could His suffering not have infinite merit? What mortal sin is so great that it could not be paid for by the death of the Son of God? What is so bloody and dirty that it could not be washed clean through the precious blood of the Son of God?

5. Do I Benefit from Christ's Death?

The afflicted person says: Christ died for everyone; but not everyone benefits from His death. How can I know that Christ's gracious work will help me? How can I be sure that I have a share in all that Christ has earned for us through His suffering and death?

The comforter says: God gives you the Word of His Gospel and in it He gives you all the grace of His Son. He stretches out His hands the whole day (Is. 65:2). He calls and invites everyone. He is certainly calling you, too. What God offers you in His mercy, grasp with the hand of faith. What you believe, you receive. Faith grasps Christ, and in Christ it grasps God's grace, the forgiveness of sins, and everlasting life.

Hear what the Word of eternal, unchangeable truth says: "For God so loved the world, that He gave His only begotten Son, that whosoever believeth in Him should not perish, but have everlasting life" (John 3:16). "He that believeth on Him is not condemned" (John 3:18), but has everlasting life. For He has given to "as many as received Him... power to become the sons of God, even to them that believe on His name" (John 1:12).

Being a child of God includes everything necessary for salvation. If we are God's children, we are born of God. It is not fleshly birth but spiritual birth that makes us God's children. If we are God's children, we have a gracious God, for a father pities his children (Ps. 103:13). If we are God's children, God has given us His Spirit.

The apostle says: "For as many as are led by the Spirit of God, they are the sons of God. For ye have not received the spirit of bondage again to fear; but ye have received the Spirit of adoption, whereby we cry, Abba, Father" (Rom. 8:14-15). He also writes: "And because ye are sons, God hath sent forth the Spirit of His Son into your hearts, crying, Abba, Father" (Gal. 4:6). Finally it is said: "And if children, then heirs; heirs of God, and joint heirs with Christ" (Rom. 8:17). For a legitimate son is also an heir.

All these precious gifts of grace are ours in Christ, Who dwells in our hearts through faith (Eph. 3:17). That is why Scripture speaks so highly of faith. "Verily, verily, I say unto you, He that heareth My Word, and believeth on Him That sent Me, hath everlasting life, and shall not come into condemnation; but is passed from death unto life. " (John 5:24). "He that believeth in Me, though he were dead, yet shall he live: And whosoever liveth and believeth in Me shall never die" (John 11:25-26).

"Whosoever believeth on Me should not abide in darkness" (John 12:46), in the darkness of ignorance, sin, and eternal death. Through the light of faith he is brought to the light of saving knowledge, true righteousness, and everlasting life.

The apostle testifies clearly that everything recorded in the Gospels about Christ's words, works, and sufferings was written for this purpose "that believing ye might have life through His name" (John 20:31). "God hath given to us eternal life, and this life is in His Son. He that hath the Son hath life" (1 John 5:11-12). But since we believe on the name of the Son of God, we know that we have eternal life (1 John 5:13).

Not only the apostles and evangelists but also all the prophets testified of Christ "that through His name whosoever believeth in Him shall receive remission of sins" (Acts 10:43). What Paul and Silas said to the jailer at Philippi, I say to you: "Believe on the Lord Jesus Christ, and thou shalt be saved" (Acts 16:31).

6. Is My Faith Genuine?

The afflicted person says: I have heard that many people falsely claim to believe and so deceive themselves. What if I am one of them? How may I be certain that my faith is saving faith and not empty deceit?

The comforter says: "Examine yourselves, whether ye be in the faith; prove your own selves. Know ye not your own selves, how that Jesus Christ is in you" (2 Cor. 13:5)? There are reliable ways to distinguish saving faith from an empty boast of faith. True faith desires to be cleansed from the corruption of sin. While faith seeks and desires forgiveness of sins, believers sense a sincere sorrow for the sins they have committed.

The Gospel is preached to the poor in spirit, who hunger and thirst after righteousness (Matt. 5:3-6; 11:5), who have a broken spirit, a broken and contrite heart (Ps. 51:17). In the mirror of the Law you will see how repulsive your sins are. You have offended God with many thoughts, words, and deeds. You have been sluggish in the fear and love of God; negligent in prayers; unfruitful in good works! How often you have followed when Satan persuaded you or the flesh seduced you or the world moved you to sin? Recognize that and sorrow for it.

If you have honest knowledge of sin in your heart, it is followed by anxiety of conscience and abhorrence of sin. If God is angry at your sins, He means it seriously. You should mourn your sins in the awareness of God's wrath. God rebukes sins strictly. So rebuke with genuine sorrow the sins you see in yourself. Recognize that God's judgment is just. Humble yourself under His powerful hand.

Do not see only your outward sins but recognize all the poison of original sin as the source of all misery. Original sin is hidden, but God reveals it (Ps. 90:8). It weakens all the powers of soul and body so that you cannot even begin, much less accomplish, anything good on your own. Through it you have become subject to death and to all the tribulation, misery, and illness that precede death.

[The answer does not seem comforting. The point is

that one who knows the seriousness of sin can hardly be hypocritical about faith. One who knows that by his sins he has deserved to suffer God's anger in hell forever will hardly take the Gospel and its comfort lightly. The comfort is knowing that if one truly feels the terror of the Law, the comfort he finds in the Gospel is also real. Trans.]

7. Repentant Sorrow

The afflicted person says: I know I was conceived and born in sin and have offended God by many various and serious sins. I know that and regret it. But maybe my sorrow is not enough, is too little for my great guilt, and is not a fully valid payment for my sins?

The comforter says: That is right. Your sorrow for sin and terror of conscience can never equal the severity of your sins. God, Whom you have offended, is infinite. Your sin is infinitely evil. The punishment for sinners in hell is infinite. How could your contrition satisfy God's infinite righteousness and appease His infinite anger?

Christ accomplished what you could not accomplish. He paid an infinite ransom for your sins. If you could pay for your own sins and blot them out with your sorrow, why would Christ have had to suffer the cross? "But Thou hast made Me to serve with thy sins, thou hast wearied Me with thine iniquities" (Is. 43:24). "I have trodden the winepress alone; and of the people there was none with Me" (Is. 63:3).

So guard against the idea that your repentant sorrow could or must equal the severity of your sins. God wants you to know your sins and to repent of them so that forgiveness can be yours by grace. It is yours when you trust Christ.

Christ preached to the meek (Is. 61:1), the humble in spirit. He heals the brokenhearted (Luke 4:18). Those who think they are healthy "need not a physician" (Matt. 9:12). Christ preached a release to the prisoners who see that they are in the spiritual prison of sin. One who claims to be free does not yearn to get out of slavery.

Christ proclaims recovery of sight to the blind, to those who mourn the spiritual blindness of their hearts. Sin remains for those who claim to see (John 9:41). Those who say, "We are rich, and increased with goods, and have need of nothing," do not know that they are "wretched, and miserable, and poor, and blind, and naked" (Rev. 3:17).

The Lord preaches freedom to broken and contrite hearts.

"The LORD killeth and maketh alive: He bringeth down to the grave, and bringeth up" (1 Sam. 2:6). He kills through the Law that brings us to repentance so that He may make alive through the comfort of the Gospel that brings us to faith. He leads to hell through the hammer of the Law so that He may lead out again through the comfort of the Gospel.

8. Terror of Conscience

The afflicted person says: I am anxious. My heart is dismayed. I see my sins all the time. They torment my conscience. I have not peace but terror before the Lord. My soul will not listen to comfort. My spirit is overwhelmed (Ps. 77:3). I have nowhere to flee for comfort.

The comforter says: Flee to Christ! He invites all who are burdened by their sins (Matt. 11:28). Hide in His wounds, and the storm of God's anger will pass over. Christ renders God favorable (Rom. 3:25). Flee to Him in faith; rest under the shadow of His wings.

"As the hart panteth after the water brooks" (Ps. 42:1), so your soul thirsts for Christ, the Source of living water. Come to Him. He will not despise you nor cast you out. He promises, "Let him that is athirst come. And whosoever will, let him take the water of life freely" (Rev. 22:17). "I will give unto him that is athirst of the fountain of the water of life freely" (Rev. 21:6).

Christ says, "Come unto Me, all ye that labour and are heavy laden, and I will give you rest" (Matt. 11:28). "Him that cometh to Me I will in no wise cast out" (John 6:37). Those are Christ's words, and His words are unchangeably true. Grasp them with a believing heart. Hold these promises before Him and seek the face of the Lord (Ps. 27:8).

Place Christ between you, the sinner, and the angry God. Appeal from the throne of God's justice to the throne of mercy in Christ. If hell makes your soul anxious, flee, to the wounds of Christ as the frightened dove flees to the clefts of the rock (Song of Sol. 2:14). Moses accuses you; ask Christ to speak for you!

Your conscience is driven back and forth; let it not be driven away from hope and trust in Christ. In the wounds of Christ you have the certain ground for trust. They overflow with streams of mercy, and they flow to you. The suffering of our Savior Jesus Christ is your refuge.

If your wisdom is foolish, if your righteousness is nothing, if you deserve only anger and punishment, Christ's suffering can help you. Saving faith is looking to Christ as He hangs on the cross, drawing from His wounds balm for one's own wounds, relying on Him with the trust of the heart and so clothing oneself in Christ's holy merit. Saving faith says:

Oh, Thou Who on the cursed tree
Didst hang, Lord Jesus, look on me,
And deep within Thy wounded side
Do Thou my guilt and sins all hide.

My wretched soul doth thirst for Thee
Till Thou forgivest, settest free;
For through my sins I die away,
But through Thy blood I live alway.

If you are troubled by your sins; if you hunger and thirst for righteousness; trust Christ. He justifies the ungodly (Rom. 4:5). If you have been justified through faith alone, you have peace with God (Rom. 5:1). Confess that you cannot attain the kingdom of heaven by your own merit; be confident that Christ possesses this kingdom for two reasons: as God's heir and also by the merit of His works. The first is enough for Him; He makes the other your own. Receive this gift; you will not be ashamed.

9. Temptation to Despair

The afflicted person says: The devil is after me to drive me to despair.

The comforter says: Despair about yourself and your own merit, for you are a sinner. But do not despair about God, Whose grace is much more powerful than sin (Rom. 5:21). Our sin compared to God's mercy is like a little spark falling into the sea. Even the ocean is limited. God's mercy has no measure.

Do not despair about Christ. He "came into the world to save sinners" (1 Tim. 1:15). His blood has far more power to appease God than sin has power to offend God. Your sins are many and great, but not so great and heavy that God cannot pardon you. God's goodness is greater than all iniquity. Sin goes down. God's grace goes up. To sin is the work of men and demons; to have mercy, to spare, to forgive are the works of God. As much more powerful as God is than men and demons, so much greater is His mercy than our sin.

"The Lord is merciful and gracious, slow to anger, and plenteous in mercy. He will not always chide: neither will He keep His anger for ever. He hath not dealt with us after our sins; nor rewarded us according to our iniquities. For as the heaven is high above the earth, so great is His mercy toward them that fear Him. As far as the east is from the west, so far hath He removed our transgressions from us" (Ps. 103:8-12).

Heaven is incomparably greater than earth. The mercy of our heavenly Father is incomparably greater than all our sins. Do not even think of saying that your iniquity is greater than the grace of the merciful God. God is far more gracious than you are sinful. God's mercy is so great that He would never condemn you even if you had all the sins of the world lying on you but repented for offending God and trusted Christ for forgiveness.

Are you forgetting the great price that Christ paid for your sins? Do you claim that your sins are greater than Christ's merit? That would make you greater than God. Your sins are great; but Christ, Who paid for your sins, is far greater. Your sins are many, but Christ suffered for you in many ways. God is infinite, and you have offended Him with your sins; but Christ is also the infinite Being, and He has reconciled you with God.

Sigh to your Father in heaven; pray in the name of His Son, your Savior: Lord God, if Thou canst not look on me because of my sins, look on me in grace because of Thy dear Son. In Him Thou art gracious to Thy servant. Look on the mystery of His flesh and forgive me the guilt of my flesh. Remember what Thy dear Son has suffered, and forget what Thy wicked servant has done.

10. Temptation to Blasphemy

The afflicted person says: At times I am tempted to blaspheme. Thoughts arise in my heart which are pure offenses against God, my Creator and Savior. I would rather die a thousand times than continue in this temptation.

The comforter says: Those thoughts are not something your heart does but something it suffers. You do not delight in them but suffer bitter pains over them. Even if some impatience of heart arises from the weakness of your flesh, the Lord knows your sighing. The burden of temptation forced harsh statements even from Job and Jeremiah. Our most gracious God has forgiven you for them.

Here you see that you have no power at all for good in yourself and learn to depend on God alone with total confidence of heart. That is the ultimate struggle against Satan. Do not lose courage! The highest Judge of battles will stand by you and will not abandon you nor fail to help you. Wait in patience and humility until you are freed from "the fiery darts of the wicked" (Eph. 6:16).

The grace of the Lord is sufficient for you (2 Cor. 12:9). The flesh lusts against the Spirit and shows itself willing to let Satan's arrows be shot at it. But the sin that dwells in your flesh is not accounted against you, the believer. By the Spirit mortify the deeds of the flesh and do not approve of blasphemous thoughts. Let those fiery darts of the wicked one be quenched by the blood of Christ. Hold the shield of faith against them.

As soon as you sense a blasphemous thought trying to arise, turn to God's Word of grace in Christ!

11. Is the Gospel for Everyone?

The afflicted person says: My heart senses some comfort. That keeps me from despair as I look at God's abundant mercy and Christ's infinite merit. But I doubt that the Gospel promise applies to me. God is not only merciful but also strict. Not all people receive Christ's benefits.

The comforter says: You are giving in to the misleading thought that the Gospel applies only to some! The Lord invites everyone, wants everyone to come to Him. He offers the Word of the Gospel and in it the benefits of Christ to everyone — not only in appearance but in earnest.

The Lord takes genuine pleasure in that. "As I live, saith the Lord GOD, I have no pleasure in the death of the wicked; but that the wicked turn from his way and live" (Ezek. 33:11; 18:32). There you hear God's sincere oath. There you hear how God desires the conversion of those who are dying in their sins by their own guilt.

"Come unto Me," says our Savior, "all ye that labour and are heavy laden, and I will give you rest" (Matt. 11:28). There you hear how the way to Christ stands open to all who are weary under the yoke of sin, how rest and refreshment are promised for their souls.

God "will have all men to be saved, and to come unto the knowledge of the truth" (1 Tim. 2:4). The apostle writes truth he learned from heaven. "For God hath concluded them all in unbelief, that He might have mercy upon all" (Rom. 11:32). There you hear again that God is concerned for the salvation of all and that the mercy of God extends to all. No one is excluded except the one who excludes himself.

There is one God for all. He wants all whom He has created to be saved. There is One Who has given Himself as the ransom for all. He wants all to benefit from this ransom. God is "not willing that any should perish, but that all should come to repentance" (2 Pet. 3:9), writes St. Peter, as he knew from his own case. There you hear that God's goodness and patience are calling all to repentance. God does not want any individual to be lost.

Do not contradict this clear truth, these words of the Holy Spirit written as bright as the light of the sun. The comfort of Scripture must mean more to you than the thoughts of your own heart. For Scripture is the Word of the living God and never deceives. It is our heart that lies and deceives.

For with Thee is the fountain of life

Psalm 36:9

12. Does God Reject Anyone Arbitrarily?

The afflicted person says: Outwardly the promise is offered to all. But maybe God has arbitrarily decided from eternity to reject some and to give them up to everlasting pain. He offers them His Word outwardly, but He does not intend to give them salvation. Maybe I am one who has been rejected.

The comforter says: An arbitrary decision of God to reject anyone is a fiction invented by some who have gone astray and lead others astray. Scripture testifies by the Word; Christ testifies by His tears; God testifies by an oath: He does not want anyone to be lost, does not desire the death of the sinner. He wants everyone to repent, know the truth, and be saved.

Can it even seem true that some are arbitrarily excluded from salvation? As God has revealed Himself in His Word, so He is in His heart. As He has shown Himself to us in Christ, His Son, so He actually is inclined toward us. Christ is the express image of the Father (Heb. 1:3), not only of His essence but also of His will.

Even the mere thought must not arise that God shows Himself outwardly gracious toward us but is inwardly nourishing flames of hatred. Be that far from God! For He Himself is indeed the truth, and all hypocrisy is an abomination to Him.

It is purely God's gift that some are saved. It is the fault of the lost themselves that they are lost. For God says: "O Israel, thou hast destroyed thyself; but in Me is thine help" (Hos. 13:9). Scripture says that man himself is the cause of damnation, and nowhere does it speak of any such arbitrary decision by God.

Since Christ really and truly, not only apparently, died for all and paid for all sin, how can anyone maintain, without blushing for shame, that God does not seriously offer the gracious deeds of His Son in the Word of the Gospel to all with the intention of bestowing salvation on them?

The atonement which Christ accomplished is valid for all without exception. That is proven by Scripture. "The LORD hath laid on Him the iniquity of us all" (Is. 53:6), the sins of all the sheep who strayed; just as the high priest laid all the sins of the whole people on the goat that was sent away into the wilderness (Lev. 16:21). The apostle repeats twice in one verse that One died for all (2 Cor. 5:15).

It was God's good pleasure "that in the dispensation of the fulness of times He might gather together in one all things in Christ, both which are in heaven, and which are on earth" (Eph. 1:9-10). "For it pleased the Father that in Him should all fulness dwell; and, having made peace through the blood of His cross, by Him to reconcile all things unto Himself; by Him, I say, whether they be things in earth, or things in heaven" (Col. 1:19-20).

Christ "gave Himself a ransom for all" (1 Tim. 2:6) whether on earth or in heaven. "For the grace of God that bringeth salvation hath appeared to all men," the grace through which Christ "gave Himself for us, that He might redeem us from all iniquity" (Titus 2:11,14). By the grace of God, Christ has tasted death for every man (Heb. 2:9).

That this ransom is valid for all without exception is proven by the general expression "world" in similar passages. "For God so loved the world, that He gave His only begotten Son,... For God sent not His Son into the world to condemn the world; but that the world through Him might be saved" (John 3:16-17). That is why He is called "the Saviour of the world" (John 4:42; 1 John 4:14).

Christ is "the Lamb of God, Which taketh away the sin of the world" (John 1:29). He gave His flesh "for the life of the world" (John 6:51). Through Him the world is reconciled to God (2 Cor. 5:19). "And He is the propitiation for our sins: and not for our's only, but also for the sins of the whole world" (1 John 2:2).

This ransom is valid for all without exception. That is proven by the distinction between the first Adam and the second Adam, Christ, as it is clearly taught by the apostle: "For if through the offense of one many be dead, much more the grace of God, and the gift by grace, which is by one Man, Jesus Christ, hath abounded unto many.... Therefore as by the offense of one judgment came upon all men to condemnation; even so by the righteousness of One the free gift came upon all men unto justification of life. For as by one man's disobedience many were made sinners, so by the obedience of One shall many be made righteous. But where sin abounded, grace did much more abound" (Rom. 5:15-20). God forbid that we should say that the sin we have inherited from Adam extends further than the grace which has been gained for us by Jesus Christ, our Savior. God forbid that we should say that Adam's disobedience has more power than Christ's obedience.

This ransom paid by Christ has universal validity. That is proven by the way Scripture speaks clearly about the damned. "Destroy not him with thy meat, for whom Christ died" (Rom. 14:15). When one uses Christian freedom at the wrong time, the weak brother perishes "for whom Christ died." "But when ye sin so against the brethren, and wound their weak conscience, ye sin against Christ" (1 Cor. 8:11-12). "There shall be false teachers among you, who privily shall bring in damnable heresies, even denying the Lord That bought them" (2 Pet. 2:1).

Those are Gospel words, apostolic words, words from God. To contradict them would be to deny Christ and to reject the benefit of His merit. So believe and do not doubt that the only-begotten Son of God came down from heaven in the last days, assumed human nature, and took away and paid for the sin of the whole world. He has borne the sins of all, and through His wounds we are all healed.

13. Can Christ's Merit Be Mine?

The afflicted person says: The merit of Christ is universal, but how can I know that His work benefits me as an individual? Much is offered to all in general that does not reach everyone in particular.

The comforter says: You can draw a valid conclusion from the general to the specific. Because God wants everyone saved, you know with certainty that He wants you saved. Because Christ died for all, you know with certainty that He died on the cross for you to cleanse you from all sin by His blood.

What is said to all in the Gospel is made your own in Absolution. When the pastor proclaims the forgiveness of sins in Jesus' name to you, you can be sure that it is valid before God in heaven. For Christ says: "Whatsoever ye shall loose on earth shall be loosed in heaven" (Matt. 18:18). "Whose soever sins ye remit, they are remitted unto them" (John 20:23).

This is the blessed ministry of reconciliation (2 Cor. 5:18) which God has entrusted to the church. This is the blessed authority of the keys which He has committed to faithful hands. This is the work of the ambassadors, which they do in Christ's stead, that God pleads through them (2 Cor. 5:20).

If something is offered to you in particular, you should not doubt that it applies to you. If in anxiety of heart you hear God's servant proclaim forgiveness of sins to you in Christ's name, you should be certain that you are hearing Christ's own Word. What is done for you in Christ's name and stead is done for you by Christ Himself. Christ Himself proclaims forgiveness of sins to you: God's servant only lends Christ His voice.

If doubt creeps into your heart, look at the words of Christ, Who says to the apostles and their successors, "He that heareth you heareth Me" (Luke 10:16). The Apostle Paul says of himself and other preachers: "We are ambassadors for Christ," in the name of Christ, in the stead of Christ, "as though God did beseech you by us; we pray you in Christ's stead, be ye reconciled to God" (2 Cor. 5:20).

"He therefore that despiseth, despiseth not man, but God, Who hath given unto us His Holy Spirit" (1 Thess. 4:8).

Christ says to you what He said to other sinners: "Thy sins are forgiven thee" (Luke 7:48; Matt. 9:2). There is no difference between the words and those the pastor says. It is not that the ones are said by a mere man and the others are said by Christ. When the pastor proclaims forgiveness to you, believe not that you hear the word of the pastor, but that you hear the Word of Christ.

14. Is the Word of Absolution True?

The afflicted person says: I see that specific comfort is given to me in Absolution; but my faith is still not firm about the promise of the Gospel. I am still tempted to despair. My flesh whispers: You hear only words; you cannot see the grace of God.

The comforter says: These words are the Word of God, Who is truthful and eternal. These words are Spirit and life (John 6:63). These words are firmer than the sky above your head or the earth beneath your feet. "Heaven and earth shall pass away: but My words shall not pass away," says Christ (Luke 21:33). "The Word of our God shall stand for ever," says the prophet (Is. 40:8). Whoever trusts this Word will also be preserved forever.

God has not only placed His Word before you but has also given you His Sacraments. They are the visible Word, visible signs of invisible grace, seals of God's promises, to nourish and strengthen your faith.

Through Baptism you have been received into God's grace, have become God's child and heir, have been cleansed by Christ's blood from your sins, have been reborn and renewed by the Holy Spirit. You have become a partaker of all heavenly blessings. For Christ has said about Baptism that it is the means of rebirth: "Except a man be born of water and of the Spirit, he cannot enter into the kingdom of God" (John 3:5). Whoever is reborn of water and the Spirit in Baptism is, according to Scripture, an heir of everlasting life. Christ said that Baptism is the means of salvation: "He that believeth and is baptized shall be saved" (Mark 16:16). The apostle says that Baptism is the washing of regeneration and renewing by the Holy Spirit (Titus 3:5) since we are baptized for the forgiveness of sins. Peter says, "Be baptized every one of you in the name of Jesus Christ for the remission of sins, and ye shall receive the gift of the Holy Ghost" (Acts 2:38).

Baptism saves us, for it is "not the putting away of the filth of the flesh, but the answer of a good conscience toward God" (1 Peter 3:21). "Be baptized, and wash away thy sins," says Ananias (Acts 22:16). Paul says, "For ye are all the children of God by faith in Christ Jesus. For as many of you as have been baptized into Christ have put on Christ" (Gal. 3:26-27). For Christ sanctifies and cleanses His church "with the washing of water by the Word" (Eph. 5:26).

From all that you can firmly conclude that Baptism means the forgiveness of sins and the new birth to the new life of faith. Baptism is the beginning of the true life and the true righteousness. It is a great washing, the Sacrament of life and salvation.

> *The Holy Ghost from heaven above*
> *Descends the watery path,*
> *And heavenly streams of grace and love*
> *Enrich the earthly bath.*
>
> *The water, as a bride, by grace*
> *Receives the Savior's Word,*
> *From seed eternal bears a race*
> *Devoted to the Lord.*
>   *(Paulinus of Nola)*

What is worked in our Baptism by God's grace is revealed in Christ's Baptism. The water has been hallowed by the Lord's body, for all that Christ earned in the body He placed into Baptism. He took Baptism upon Himself with us sinners to testify that we would become His members through Baptism.

As the eternal Father said at Jesus' Baptism: "This is My beloved Son" (Matt. 3:17), so He still accepts as His children all who believe and are baptized. As heaven opened at Jesus' Baptism, so for us still the door to paradise is opened by this Sacrament. As at the Baptism of Christ the Holy Spirit descended upon Him in the form of a dove, so the Holy Spirit is present in our Baptism and powerfully works our rebirth and renewal.

So the following are active together in Baptism: The grace of the Father, Who accepts us as His children; the merit of the Son, Who cleanses us; and the work of the Holy Spirit, Who gives us the new birth.

So if you have been baptized, you should never more doubt

the grace of God, the forgiveness of sins, and the promise of salvation. Baptism is the washing of regeneration; but where there is regeneration, there is the forgiveness of sins, there is God's grace, there is perfect righteousness, there is renovation, there is the gift of the Holy Spirit, there is adoption, there is the inheritance of everlasting life.

15. The Baptismal Covenant

The afflicted person says: I believe that through Baptism I have been accepted into the covenant of God's grace, have received the forgiveness of sins, and have been written in the book of life. But by my sins I have fallen from grace, have lost forgiveness by committing new sins, and have deserved to be erased from the book of life.

The comforter says: God's covenant is everlasting; the return to it in repentance always stands open. God says that circumcision is an everlasting covenant (Gen. 17:13). We should not doubt that in Baptism, too, God establishes an everlasting covenant, for Baptism has replaced circumcision (Col. 2:11).

The Lord says, "I will betroth thee unto Me for ever; yea, I will betroth thee unto Me in righteousness, and in judgment, and in lovingkindness, and in mercies" (Hos. 2:19-20). "For the mountains shall depart, and the hills be removed; but My kindness shall not depart from thee, neither shall the covenant of My peace be removed, saith the LORD that hath mercy on thee" (Is. 54:10). So God forbid that we should say that our unbelief can make God's faithfulness of no effect (Rom. 3:3).

Even if we deny faith and His Word, God remains faithful, truthful, and unchangeable. He cannot deny Himself (2 Tim. 2:13). Through your sins of weakness you do not fall from God's covenant of grace. Through sins of malice, stubbornly committed contrary to your conscience, you will fall from God's grace. But the return to this everlasting covenant of God stands open in repentance. Peter had denied Christ; but when he turned again, he sought just as much in Baptism the promise of salvation (1 Pet. 3:21).

The Galatians and the Corinthians had fallen very seriously. But when they had repented, the apostle comforted them by referring to their Baptism. He says: "For as many of you as have been baptized into Christ have put on Christ" (Gal. 3:27). He says clearly that they have been washed and have been baptized into one spiritual body (1 Cor. 12:13). So it is made clear that the power of Baptism reaches into the future and is not destroyed by backsliding. From God's side the promise remains firm and valid.

Paul says that Christ cleanses the church with the washing of water by the Word. Through Baptism and the Word all sin is washed away from those who are born again, not only past sins but also those which will be committed later in ignorance or weakness. It is not that Baptism is to be repeated each time one sins, but that through it the forgiveness which was once bestowed can be received by the believer not only for previous sins but also for subsequent sins.

Recognize and mourn your sins, but do not deny or forget the grace which has been given to you in Baptism. Even if you fall a thousand times, turn back again and again. "Return, thou backsliding Israel, saith the LORD; and I will not cause mine anger to fall upon you: I am merciful, saith the LORD, and I will not keep anger for ever" (Jer. 3:12). Let your heart hold this word before the Lord (Ps. 27:7). He will have mercy on you and remember His promise; for He cannot deny Himself and His Word.

"He saved us by the washing in which the Holy Spirit gives us a new birth . . ."

Titus 3:5

16. The Assurance of Grace

The afflicted person says: How can I be sure that God has accepted me back into Baptismal grace? If that could be confirmed to my heart by a firm and certain seal! If there were another Sacrament through which that promise of grace could be sealed to me!

The comforter says: In the Lord's Supper you receive the body which Christ gave into death for you and the blood which Christ shed on the cross for your sins. Since in the holy Supper you receive the payment by which you have been redeemed, the body and blood of Christ, you can be sure that you share in all that Christ earned for you on the altar of the cross: the grace of God, the forgiveness of sins, righteousness, life, and salvation.

How can you doubt that you have been accepted back into God's grace? What is closer to the Father than His only-begotten Son? He is in the bosom of the Father (John 1:18). He is in the Father and the Father in Him (John 14:10). He and the Father are One (John 10:30). What is closer to the Son of God than His flesh and blood and the human nature which He has taken on? He has entered into union with it. If you eat Christ's body and drink His blood, you are intimately united with God. Christ abides in you and you in Him. What is brought closer to us than what we eat and drink? As often as you eat the life-giving body of Christ and drink His precious blood, you receive spiritual life from Him, the Source of life. Christ has taken on human nature. In it He blotted out sin, destroyed death, created our life anew, and filled it with all the fullness of grace and heavenly wealth. This human nature, which He took on, which he renewed, sanctified, and filled with heavenly wealth, He wants to give back to you, so that you are sure that all the wealth of this holy Supper applies to you.

He plants your poor, corrupt nature into His holy, life giving body, so that you receive from it an antidote to the spiritual poison in your nature. He is the Vine; we are the branches. Whoever abides in Him brings forth much fruit (John 15:5). The impurity of your human nature is covered by the body and blood of Christ which you receive. It cannot happen that your body remains in the grave after it has been nourished with the body and blood of Christ. Even the bones of the dead Elisha gave life (2 Kings 13:21). How much more will the body of the living and life-giving Christ be able to awaken you to everlasting life?

17. Worthy Reception of the Lord's Supper

The afflicted person says: I know that believers receive these blessings by the proper use of the Lord's Supper. But I am afraid, for the apostle says: "Whosoever shall eat this bread, and drink this cup of the Lord, unworthily, shall be guilty of the body and blood of the Lord" (1 Cor. 11:27). I am afraid that I could receive this heavenly meal unworthily.

The comforter says: Through recognizing and regretting your unworthiness you avoid receiving the Sacrament unworthily. The apostle does not say that those who are weak in faith receive the Sacrament unworthily. Instead, the Sacrament was instituted to strengthen faith and to comfort the weak.

Those who receive it unworthily are those who do not examine themselves and do not recognize the Lord's body (1 Cor. 11:28-29); those who, without repentance and faith, without horror of sin and the intention to live better, come to the holy Supper as to an ordinary meal; those who do not distinguish this heavenly meal from common food; those who do not recognize its majesty and do not bring with them the due preparation of the heart. Such recipients sin just as much against the body and blood of Christ by unworthy eating and drinking as those who crucified Him sinned against Him.

God forbid that you should count yourself among them. For you recognize the filth of your sins and mourn the impurity of your human nature. You consider the greatness of what is given and promised you in the holy Supper. You hunger and thirst after righteousness, and you will also be filled (Matt. 5:6). Sins cannot harm you, for they no longer please you. You run with tears to your heavenly Father (Luke 15:20, 22-23). You mourn your sins and long to have the hunger of your soul stilled with this heavenly food.

Do not doubt that the gracious and merciful Father will run to you (Luke 15:20-24). He will kiss you and receive you with joy. He will give you "the best robe" of Christ's innocence and put on you the clothing of salvation. He will put the ring on your hand and seal you with His Holy Spirit. He will put shoes on your feet and lead you on the way of peace and righteousness. He will satisfy you with the flesh of the Sacrifice that was offered on the altar of the cross and has been brought to Himself as a sweet-smelling aroma.

Do not fear at all that you receive the meal unworthily. He who is totally unworthy in his own eyes is acceptable to God. He who displeases himself pleases God. He who is smitten within himself and brokenhearted is lifted up by the merciful hand of God.

The Holy Supper

Strong & Sure Medicine

18. My Faith Is Weak

The afflicted person says: Faith is necessary to receive the blessings of the Word and the Sacraments. To receive any gift, there must be not only a giving hand but also a receiving hand. But my faith is very weak. My heart is tossed back and forth by various temptations. It is often shaken, and I am deprived of the firmness of confidence.

The comforter says: Weak faith is still faith. Faith grasps Christ and in Christ the grace of God, the forgiveness of sins, and everlasting life, not because it is strong but because it is faith. A strong faith grasps Christ more firmly, but a weak faith still grasps Christ for salvation.

Your Savior, Jesus Christ, will not break a bruised reed nor quench a smoking flax (Is. 42:3). He graciously accepts the one weak in faith (Rom. 14:3). The smallest spark of faith is a work of the Holy Spirit, for we are not "sufficient of ourselves to think any thing as of ourselves" (2 Cor. 3:5). God works both the willing and the doing (Phil. 2:13). God will not despise the work He has begun in your heart but will complete and confirm it (Phil. 1:6).

God wants to comfort us as a mother comforts her child (Is. 66:13). But a mother deals much more tenderly with a little child that cannot speak, and takes greater care with him than with a grown child. God does not cast away the one who is weak in faith but takes great pains to heal and strengthen him, as we do for one who is physically weak.

Jesus says, "If ye have faith as a grain of mustard seed, ye shall say unto this mountain, Remove hence to yonder place; and it shall remove; and nothing shall be impossible unto you" (Matt. 17:20). If miracle-working faith can move mountains although it is no larger than a mustard seed, saving faith can remove mountains of temptation and doubt although it is weak. The power of God is mighty in us who are weak (2 Cor. 12:9).

Guard against losing courage because of the weakness of your faith and look rather to God's power. God can make fruitful what is barren; heal what is wounded; bend what is rigid; warm what is cold; set right what has gone wrong. Recognize the weakness of your faith and lean that much more heavily on the staff of the divine Word. The Word is the seed from which faith grows, and it is also that which nourishes faith. Pray with Christ's disciples: "Lord, increase our faith!" (Luke 17:5), and with the father of the possessed boy: "Lord, I believe; help Thou mine unbelief" (Mark 9:24).

19. Faith and Feelings

The afflicted person says: My faith is weak. Sometimes I do not feel it at all in my heart and do not call on God with the fervor to reach heaven. I fear I have lost my faith, that it is extinguished. If faith is extinguished, what hope, what salvation remains for me? I am examining myself whether I am in the faith (2 Cor. 13:5), and I feel no faith in my heart.

The comforter says: The Holy Spirit helps us in our weakness. "For we know not what we should pray for as we ought: but the Spirit Itself maketh intercession for us with groanings which cannot be uttered" (Rom. 8:26). At times we do not feel what we believe or how we believe, but the Spirit nourishes and preserves faith in our hearts.

The spark may lie hidden under the ashes. Faith sometimes dwells in secret comers of the heart, even if we do not feel it. Never conclude from the fact that you do not feel your faith that it has ceased to exist. You still have the desire. You sigh and want to believe. Even this desire, this sighing, this willing comes from faith.

These are two different things: To feel nothing of one's faith and not to want to believe. In the one case it is a matter of struggling. In the other case it is a matter of stiff-necked malice.

Christ dwells in your heart by faith (Eph. 3:17) even if you do not feel His presence. The Holy Spirit, the Comforter, also dwells in your heart even if you do not always feel His comfort. As Abraham, the father of believers, believed in hope against hope (Rom. 4:18), you should also rely on the Word when there is nothing to feel.

Every thought must be brought into captivity to Christ (2 Cor. 10:5). Take this lack of feeling captive under faith. Take the Word with your heart and keep firmly hanging onto it! The seed lies hidden under the soil of the earth before it has brought forth visible ears. The seed of faith lies hidden in the heart even when no fruit has yet shown itself openly.

In sleep you feel nothing of your faith, but no one can say that your faith has ceased to be. In this temptation, a sleep has overtaken your soul so that you cannot feel the stirrings of your faith. God forbid that you should think for that reason that your faith is totally extinquished.

20. I Cannot Believe

The afflicted person says: I sigh to my Savior, but I feel that I cannot believe. That causes me sorrow. I would like to be able to receive the grace of Christ, but I am unable to grasp it in faith.

The comforter says: By yourself you are unable, but you can do all things through Christ Who strengthens you (Phil. 4:13). It is God's will that you believe. He gives you His Word and uses it to kindle faith in your heart by the power of the Holy Spirit. Do not give up on the Word. Do not look elsewhere. You will soon sense the rich fruit of the Word.

God wants you to believe. He works faith in you. Do not maliciously oppose His will. You say that you cannot believe. Yet you must confess that you sigh for Christ and desire His grace. This desire is the beginning of faith. The Holy Spirit will complete the good work of faith which He has begun in you. You need not doubt His blessed work!

You cannot expect a feeling of the faith that is kindled in your heart before you have joy in the Word of the Gospel. In the school of the Holy Spirit the beginning must be made by hearing the Word of God. Through it one is brought to faith, and though faith one receives a feeling of his faith. If you say you cannot believe, hear and learn the Word so that you believe.

God gives the Holy Spirit to those who ask Him (Luke 11:13), and yet without the Holy Spirit we cannot ask at all. God gives faith to those who sigh for Him, and yet this sighing is impossible without a beginning in faith. Faith arises with a struggle in the heart, increases with a struggle in the heart, is completed with a struggle in the heart. What we cannot do of ourselves we can do through the gift of Him Who has said: "No man can come to Me, except the Father Which hath sent Me draw him.... Every man therefore that hath heard, and hath learned of the Father, cometh unto Me.... And him that cometh to Me I will in no wise cast out" (John 6:44, 45, 37). God is drawing you through His Word. Hear and learn. You will be strengthened in faith in Christ.

21. I Do So Few Good Works

The afflicted person says: Living faith is active in love (Gal. 5:6). But the number of my good works, which could give a clear testimony to my faith, is not at all large. "I find then a law that, when I would do good, evil is present with me.... For to will is present with me; but how to perform that which is good I find not" (Rom. 7:21, 18).

The comforter says: You are right to evaluate the light of faith by the rays of good works. As the works which do not come from faith are not truly good works, so the faith which does not have works is not proper faith but a deceitful image. "Let your light so shine before men, that they may see your good works," says the Savior (Matt. 5:16).

The evaluation of faith by works should follow the understanding that faith results in new obedience while repentance is its forerunner and trust in Christ is its substance. So you are right to judge the light of faith by the rays of good works.

But be careful not to think that only those works are good which are great in outward appearance, in the eyes of people, and are completely free of the stains of sin that still adheres to you. By good works we should mainly understand the internal renewal of the heart and spiritual stirrings which are kindled by the Holy Spirit in the hearts of the regenerate. That is why holy thoughts, good intentions, true fear of God, upright love, and fervent prayer are good works even if they do not outwardly impress people.

The outward works only give testimony to the internal glory of renewal. If you have nothing else to offer God, bring Him the will and intention to live a godly life. Bring God your heart, and you have offered everything. If you lack the eternal power to do such works, your internal good will pleases God.

It is not as if you could hope to be free of all weakness in this life. Our good works do not please God because they are good, but because they come from faith in Christ and are offered by God's dear children as sacrifices of thanksgiving. Recognize that good works give a testimony to your faith so that you do not become despondent; but also recognize that they are nothing perfect and that the stain of sin adheres to them, so that you do not become arrogant.

22. What Merit Do I Have?

The afflicted person says: God is just, and His judgments are just. He will not give everlasting life to anyone who has not earned it by good works. How can I have hope? My supposedly good works are not at all meritorious. By my own works I have deserved nothing but punishment.

The comforter says: Everlasting life is not a payment for our works but a gracious gift of God in Christ Jesus (Rom. 6:23) and for Christ's sake. We cannot do anything to put God into our debt so that He would owe us everlasting life. All saints confess that before God no one is guiltless (Rom. 3:23); that all their righteousnesses are as filthy rags (Is. 64:6); that no one can stand if God wills to account sin (Ps. 130:3); that even when they have done all that God has commanded them, they are unprofitable servants (Luke 17:10).

How can there be any talk of merit here? Who can maintain that his righteousness or holiness suffices for salvation? Our works as well as our sufferings "are not worthy to be compared with the glory which shall be revealed in us" (Rom. 8:18).

We cannot earn a crumb of the bread that we eat but must beg it from God in daily prayer. How much less will we be able to merit everlasting life? If you want to lose grace, then boast about your merits! God gives out of pure grace. He saves out of pure grace. He finds nothing in us that deserves salvation and a great deal that deserves damnation. Death is called wages, but everlasting life is called a gift of grace (Rom. 6:23). Wages are paid, but a gift is given. Let others look for merit. You look for grace! Trust Christ alone. Grasp His mercy. Seek merit only in His wounds, and you will need no merit of your own.

23. The Law Accuses Me

The afflicted person says: I see that our works do not reconcile God nor earn salvation. They please God only because they come from faith. But they must still anger Him, for they do not fully agree with His Law! The Law is an unchangeable standard of righteousness and condemns everything that does not agree with it. Damnation threatens me like an arrow in flight unless you show me what kind of shield I can hold up against it.

The comforter says: "Christ hath redeemed us from the curse of the Law, being made a curse for us: for it is written, Cursed is every one that hangeth on a tree" (Gal. 3:13). "But when the fullness of time was come, God sent forth His Son, made of a woman, made under the Law, to redeem them that there were under the Law, that we might receive the adoption of sons" (Gal. 4:4-5). "Christ is the end [fulfillment] of the Law for righteousness to everyone that believeth" (Rom. 10:4). So there is no condemnation to fear for you and all who are in Christ through faith (Rom. 8:1).

"For the Law of the Spirit of life in Christ Jesus hath made me free from the Law of sin and death. For what the Law could not do, in that it was weak through the flesh, God sending His own Son in the likeness of sinful flesh, and for sin, condemned sin in the flesh: that the righteousness of the Law might be fulfilled in us, who walk not after the flesh, but after the Spirit" (Rom. 8:2-4). If you receive the work of Christ in faith, you have no reason to fear the curse of the Law.

"The sting of death is sin; and the strength of sin is the Law. But thanks be to God, Which giveth us the victory through our Lord Jesus Christ" (1 Cor. 15:56-57). By His death He has conquered our death. By His suffering He has fully paid for our sins. By His obedience He has perfectly fulfilled the Law in our place.

The Law has not been uprooted but only transplanted. Law and Gospel do not nullify each other, for the Law is not against the promises of God (Gal. 3:21) since it is much rather established through faith (Rom. 3:31). The Gospel says that what the Law requires of us has been accomplished by Christ in our place. What the Law needs are Jesus' deeds [Was das Gesetz verlangt, wird durch Christum erlangtl].

The Law condemns sin and condemns us because of sin. But Christ suffered the penalty and paid the price for our sins. He gives us His righteousness. The Law has been fulfilled by Christ's perfect obedience. Christ's fulfillment of the Law can benefit us because He was not obligated to do it.

You should not see your death in your body but in Christ, the Conqueror of death, Who gives life and salvation. You should not see your sin on your conscience but on Christ, the Lamb of God, Who takes away your sin and the sin of the whole world. You should not see hell and the anxiety of everlasting damnation coming to you but to Christ, Who on the cross took upon Himself the anxiety of damnation and conquered it. You should not see the Law as being against yourself but as it has been fulfilled by Christ and was nailed with Him to the cross.

"The Cross is Something Foolish to Those Who Perish But It is Gods Power to Us Who are Saved"
(1 Corinthians 1:18)

24. My Conscience Accuses Me

The afflicted person says: In addition to the accusation of the Law there is the testimony of my conscience. This judge accuses me even if no one else brings any charge against me. I cannot escape from the judge at home. Many sins are written truthfully in the book of my conscience. I view them with horror. I am miserable. Who will save me from this court where I myself am the accused, the accuser, and the prosecution witness all in one?

The comforter says: "For if our heart condemn us, God is greater than our heart" (1 John 3:20). Though the memory of past sins accuses you, Christ is still your Redeemer. He has paid for your sins. He declares you free and makes you free. He has saved you. He has blotted out "the handwriting of ordinances that was against us, which was contrary to us, and took it out of the way, nailing it to His cross" (Col. 2:14). The writing in your conscience that accuses you was nailed to the cross. It is invalid and powerless before God.

"Therefore being justified by faith, we have peace with God through our Lord Jesus Christ" (Rom. 5:1). Peace for the conscience, rest for the heart, and blessed calm for the soul — Christ, the Conqueror of death, sin, and the devil, has brought these with Him from the grave and has given them to all who believe in Him. When you sense the nagging of your conscience, smother it immediately by sincere repentance, pray that God will give you peace of heart and the forgiveness of sins for Jesus' sake, and guard against new wounds in the conscience, against backsliding into the old sins.

In this life there is still time to quiet the conscience. The book of conscience can still be corrected from the book of life. But at the last judgment the books will be open (Rev. 20:12). In them there will be written in large letters for all to read all the sins of those who have not received forgiveness for Jesus' sake through faith. Before the day of judgment arrives and the time of grace is past, you still have precious hope and certain confidence. "How much more shall the blood of Christ, Who through the eternal Spirit offered Himself without spot to God, purge your conscience from dead works to serve the living God?" (Heb. 9:14).

25. My Repentance Comes Too Late

The afflicted person says: I am truly sorry that my conscience has suffered so many wounds. I want these wounds to be healed. I want to keep a good conscience in the future. But I am afraid that my repentance comes too late. I have often despised the grace of God and am afraid that I could be despised in return.

The comforter says: As long as one is still living in this world, repentance cannot be too late. Many are hired for the Lord's vineyard at the eleventh hour and receive the reward of grace (Matt. 20:9). No delay can limit God's love for people. Repentance is never too late for God, for in His eyes the past and the future are always the same as the present.

Look at the thief on the cross. The dying man still had time. He confessed Christ. He received the forgiveness of sins and the promise of the heavenly paradise.

"While it is called today" (Heb. 3:13), God earnestly desires our conversion. As long as the heavenly Bridegroom delays His arrival (Matt. 25:5), the door of grace and forgiveness stands open. The whole lifetime, even the very last hour, is given to us as time for repentance. God spreads out His hands all the day (Is. 65:2). Whoever comes to Him, whenever he comes, Jesus will never cast out (John 6:37). You need never fear that true repentance comes too late.

Do not repent only because death is drawing near. Do not repent only because you fear a punishment drawing near. True repentance comes from God's Law, through which the Holy Spirit brings you to regret your many sins because by them you have offended God the Lord.

Trust Christ who died to forgive your sins. The good news of forgiveness creates the desire to spend the rest of your life serving God. Humble yourself before the Lord. God will not despise a broken and contrite heart (Psalm 51:17). He says: "But to this man will I look, even to him that is poor and of a contrite spirit, and trembleth at My Word" (Is. 66:2).

26. Is God Gracious?

The afflicted person says: I have true repentance in my heart for my sins. I do not entirely doubt God's mercy. But my heart is still tossed around by waves of doubt. I am not yet certain about the forgiveness of sins by grace. I hope for the best, but I also doubt in my lowliness. Considering God's mercy lifts me up. But the thought of my unworthiness strikes me down.

The comforter says: Your wavering faith needs firm support so that you can stand against all the storms of doubt. Such doubt is not a humble confession of unworthiness but a dangerous contradiction to the faith we ought to have in God's promises. Even in a case of late conversion and repentance, doubt has no valid excuse at all. God's grace in Christ promises the forgiveness of sins to all believers.

Remember the unchangeable truth of God's promises. God has promised His grace, the forgiveness of sins, and everlasting life to everyone who repents for sin and seeks forgiveness in Christ. These believers will want to amend their sinful lives with God's help. All who believe in the Son are not lost but have everlasting life (John 3:15). "He that believeth on Him is not condemned" (John 3:18). "He that hath the Son hath life" (1 John 5:12). "He that believeth and is baptized shall be saved" (Mark 16:16). The One Who has promised that is God, Whose Word stands firmer than heaven and earth, Who is truth itself, Who is faithful and cannot deny Himself (2 Tim. 2:13).

What God offers you with firm promises, receive in faith and do not make your weakness an excuse for not confidently grasping God's promises. Even this frailty of your nature is to be healed by the power of the Holy Spirit. You believe in Christ not out of natural power but through the work of the Holy Spirit. By the gracious work of the Holy Spirit, you may be certain of God's mercy and overcome all doubt that still adheres to your corrupt nature.

"He that believeth not God hath made Him a liar" (1 John 5:10). To the extent that you doubt, you still lack confidence. Fight against such doubt and do not act as if it were humility.

That only sounds good. We should admittedly be humble in view of our unworthiness. But in considering God's promises we should have very firm confidence. God revealed His will in His Word so that we would have certainty about His will.

"God of God has taken our sufferings upon Himself..." Athanasius

God has given the Law promises, which can be received only on a condition which we cannot meet, the condition of perfect obedience. But God has also given the Gospel promises out

of pure grace so that we rely on them in firm trust of the heart. The apostle says: "Therefore it is of faith, that it might be by grace; to the end the promise might be sure" (Rom. 4:16). Human promises are uncertain and doubtful. "All men are liars" (Ps. 116:11). But God's promises are certain and unchanging, for God is truth itself. As God is truthful when he threatens, so He is truthful when He promises. Without Christ all who do not repent and believe face certain damnation. In Christ all believers are promised certain salvation.

Or do you doubt that what God has promised will happen? His Word stands forever firm. If an honest man promised you something, you would trust his promise and not worry that he was deceiving you. You know that he will keep his word and do what he has said. Now God speaks with you, and you waver so untrustingly with a doubting heart?

But remember that God's oath stands firm. "As I live, saith the Lord GOD, I have no pleasure in the death of the wicked; but that the wicked turn from his way and live" (Ezek. 33:11). Christ says, "Verily, verily, I say unto you, He that heareth My Word and believeth on Him That sent Me, hath everlasting life, and shall not come into condemnation; but is passed from death unto life" (John 5:24). "Verily, verily, I say unto you, If a man keep My saying, he shall never see death" (John 8:51). God has said that. God has promised that. If that is still too little for you, He has also sworn it. How blessed we are that God swears for our sakes! But how very miserable we are if we do not believe Him even when He swears.

God's wondrous, glorious mercy can never be praised enough: "Wherein God, willing more abundantly to shew unto the heirs of promise the immutability of His counsel, confirmed it by an oath: that by two immutable things, in which it was impossible for God to lie, we might have a strong consolation, who have fled for refuge to lay hold upon the hope set before us" (Heb. 6:17-18).

27. I Am Not Ready to Die

The afflicted person says: But are these promises firm and unchangeable for me, too? Am I one of those to whom God promises and gives such great things that I can be ready to die in confidence and faith?

The comforter says: God makes these promises to all who take refuge in Christ. God promises it to you, for you believe in Christ. Look again at the inward testimony of the Holy Spirit — the fact that He has brought you to faith in Christ.

The Holy Spirit gives you His testimony not only outwardly in His Word but also inwardly in your heart. "The Spirit Itself beareth witness with our spirit, that we are the children of God: and if children, then heirs; heirs of God" (Rom. 8:16-17). "Now we have received... the Spirit Which is of God; that we might know the things that are freely given to us of God" (1 Cor. 2:12).

It is God Who gives strength and power to you and all believers in Christ. He has anointed you. He has sealed you and given you the pledge of the Spirit in your heart (2 Cor. 5:5). "And because ye are sons, God hath sent forth the Spirit of His Son into your hearts, crying, Abba, Father" (Gal. 4:6). "In Whom ye also trusted, after that ye heard the Word of truth, the Gospel of your salvation: in Whom also after that ye believed, ye were sealed with that Holy Spirit of promise, Which is the earnest of our inheritance until the redemption of the purchased possession" (Eph. 1:13-14).

With the Holy Spirit "ye are sealed unto the day of redemption" (Eph. 4:30). As a fiancé, who has promised marital faithfulness to his fiancée, gives her a ring to seal his promise to marry her, God has betrothed you to Himself in mercy (Hos. 2:19). But the marriage of the Lamb (Rev. 19:7) has not yet come. That is why He gives you the pledge of the Holy Spirit, so that through Him you become certain that He will fulfill His promises and some day go with you to the heavenly wedding.

The Holy Spirit is the Spirit of adoption, for He testifies to you that God has accepted you as His child. He is the Seal through Which God's promises are sealed to your heart. He is the Pledge, through Whom the Word of truth is confirmed to you. "Hereby know we that we dwell in Him, and He in us, because He hath given us of His Spirit" (1 John 4:13).

Our Citizenship is in Heaven (Philippians 3:20)

28. Does the Holy Spirit Dwell in Me?

The afflicted person says: How can I be certain that my heart is a temple and dwelling of the Holy Spirit? Sin adheres to me. I know that nothing good dwells in my flesh (Rom. 7:18). How can the Holy Spirit dwell in me?

The comforter says: In this life we receive only the first fruits of the Spirit (Rom. 8:23). In everlasting life we will receive the full measure of the whole harvest. In this life there is always the battle between flesh and spirit, and we remain in part still "carnal, sold under sin" (Rom. 7:14). At the same time we are also temples of the Holy Spirit since the gracious blessing of renewal has begun in us.

You can recognize that the Spirit of God dwells in you: you mourn sin and want to avoid it; you believe in Christ, for the Holy Spirit is the Spirit of faith (2 Cor. 4:13); you call upon God the Father of mercy, for He is the Spirit of grace and prayer (Zech. 12:10) and calls out in the hearts of the believers, "Abba, Father" (Gal. 4:6); you desire what is good, for those who are temples of the Holy Spirit are led by Him (Rom. 8:14); and you sometimes sense in your heart a foretaste of everlasting life, "For the kingdom of God is not meat and drink; but righteousness, and peace, and joy in the Holy Spirit" (Rom. 14:17).

In your soul the Spirit of the Son cries in you: "Abba, Father." You can be certain that you share in God's fatherly love since you are moved by the Spirit of the Son. Although that may sometimes be weak, do not let your courage sink. Pray for an increase of the Spirit, for God will "give the Holy Spirit to them that ask Him" (Luke 11:13). Stir up the gift of the Holy Spirit Which is in you (2 Tim. 1:6) by asking, seeking, and knocking (Matt. 7:7-8); and by hearing and learning the Word. This life is not perfect but is a journey toward perfection.

In addition to this inward testimony of the Holy Spirit, God has given you the Sacraments. They are seals of divine promises, bearers of the blessings of Christ, and means to awaken, nourish, and confirm faith so that you may be certain that the grace of God applies to you. Through Baptism you have been accepted into God's grace. In the holy Supper you are fed with the body and blood of Christ. In private Absolution you are declared free from the bonds of your sin.

Believe the Word of the Gospel firmly. Why do you doubt and waver? That means wanting to know nothing of God; that means offending Christ, the Teacher of the faith, by the sin of unbelief; that means standing in the church and yet lacking faith in the house of faith.

God is not deceiving when He promises that He will hear your prayer and that what we ask according to His will shall be given to us. "Verily, verily, I say unto you, Whatsoever ye shall ask the Father in My name, He will give it you" (John 16:23). "If two of you shall agree on earth as touching any thing that they shall ask, it shall be done for them of My Father Which is in heaven" (Matt. 18:19). "This is the confidence that we have in Him, that, if we ask any thing according to His will, He heareth us" (1 John 5:14).

God, Who has promised to hear us, has commanded us to pray for forgiveness. What reason is there still to doubt the forgiveness of sins? How could Christ have taught us to put the little word "Amen" after the prayer if He had wanted us to doubt that we would be heard?

Note the character of faith! "We have access by faith into this grace wherein we stand, and rejoice in hope of the glory of God" (Rom. 5:2). Through faith we may "come boldly unto the throne of grace, that we may obtain mercy, and find grace to help in time of need" (Heb. 4:16). We "are kept by the power of God through faith unto salvation" (1 Pet. 1:5). Through faith "we know that we have passed from death unto life" (1 John 3:14). Through faith we are "persuaded, that neither death, nor life, nor angels, nor principalities, nor powers, nor things present, nor things to come, nor height, nor depth, nor any other creature, shall be able to separate us from the love of God, which is in Christ Jesus our Lord" (Rom. 8:38-39).

Christ has promised that where He is, you will also be

(John 14:3). God promised that you will live forever. And you do not believe? But God has already done more than He has promised. He has died for you. It is harder to believe that the Eternal One should die than that the mortal one should live forever. You already hold firmly to what is harder to believe. Why are you still doubting the other? God has promised you, heaven. He has given you the Son, Who is a gift greater than heaven and earth.

29. Will I Persevere in the Faith?

The afflicted person says: I do not doubt that access to God stands open through Christ. But I doubt that I will persevere. "He that endureth to the end shall be saved" (Matt. 10:22). Among Christians one asks not about the beginning but about the end. Judas began well but ended poorly, while Paul began poorly but ended well. Without perseverance a soldier does not come to victory. Our Savior cries out: "Hold that fast which thou hast, that no man take thy crown" (Rev. 3:11). I hear that and am afraid. I fear and doubt. I doubt, and the confidence of my heart is gone.

The comforter says: Look at these three: God's love that accepts you as a child; God's truth that keeps its promises; God's power that gives what He has promised. Your foolish thoughts may grumble as much as they want. If they say: "Who are you? How great is the future glory? How do you intend to earn it?" answer with all confidence, "I know Whom I have believed" (2 Tim. 1:12), that He in love has made me His child; that He is truthful in promising and powerful in giving. That is the firm anchor of your hope.

These are the three pillars on which you can be supported against all the waves and floods of doubt: The gracious will of God, Who makes you His child; the reliable faithfulness, with which He gives you His promises; and the immeasurable power with which He fulfills them.

Your God is good and has promised you good. "He which hath begun a good work in you will perform it" according to His good pleasure (Phil. 1:6; 2:13). Your God is good and has promised you good. He Who has promised it is also faithful and truthful, "Who will not suffer you to be tempted above that ye are able; but will with the temptation also make a way to escape, that ye may be able to bear it" (1 Cor. 10:13). Your God is good and has promised you good. He Who has promised is also powerful to fulfill His promises.

You can be certain that He is able to keep that which you

have committed to Him until Judgment Day (2 Tim. 1:12). No one shall pluck Christ's sheep out of His hand. The Father in heaven has given the Son for you, and no one can pluck them out of the Father's hand (John 10:28-29).

Christ, the only High Priest of the New Testament, has prayed for all who believe in Him through the Word, that they might be with Him and see the glory which the Father in heaven has given Him (John 17:20). Since you believe in Christ, you have the testimony of God in yourself (1 John 5:10).

Christ has prayed for you. Can you doubt that His prayer will be heard by the Father in heaven? The Son, Who is in the bosom of the Father (John 1:18), should not be heard by the Father? God forbid! The Son, in Whom the Father is pleased (Matt. 3:17), should be denied His request? God forbid! Christ has prayed for you with a prayer that will be heard, that you will live with Him and some day partake of heavenly glory.

The Name of the Lord
Is a Strong Tower
(Proverbs 18:10)

30. The Devil's Deceit and Power

The afflicted person says: I hope that I will be recognized as a faithful lamb in the Good Shepherd's hand. But I am afraid of the deceit of Satan, who "as a roaring lion, walketh about, seeking whom he may devour" (1 Pet. 5:8). I am afraid of his power, for he is an enemy bold, strong, clever, skillful, tireless, zealous, quick to attack, full of tricks, and experienced in strategy. How can I guard against his deceit and flee his power? First he acts openly and forcefully, then sweetly and deceitfully. But he always attacks and persecutes me with malice and horror.

The comforter says: Christ says that no one will pluck His sheep out of His hand (John 10:28). Not even the wolf of hell can do it, no matter how well-equipped he is to harm us. The prince of this world has nothing in Christ (John 14:30). So he has nothing in those who are in Christ through faith and in whose hearts Christ dwells by faith (Eph. 3:17). Christ fights for you and in you. Trust Him! The devil cannot be stronger than God the Son. Christ was tempted by the devil (Matt. 4:1) and triumphed mightily. The victory of the Lord is the triumph of His servants.

"Through death" Christ destroyed "him that had the power of death, that is, the devil" (Heb. 2:14). "Having spoiled principalities and powers, He made a shew of them in it [the cross]" (Col. 2:15). By the cross the heavenly David conquered the hellish Goliath. Christ's battle and victory means the salvation of the whole church. We will sing the victory and triumph song: "Now is come salvation, and strength, and the kingdom of our God, and the power of His Christ: for the accuser of our brethren is cast down, which accused tqem before our God day and night. And they overcame him by the blood of the Lamb and by the Word of their testimony" (Rev. 12:10-11). You should set all your confidence and all your hope of glory on this victory in Christ.

The Lord lifts you up when you are weak and crowns you when you have conquered. "Be strong in the Lord, and in the power of His might. Put on the whole armour of God, that ye may be able to stand against the wiles of the devil. For we wrestle not against flesh and blood, but against principalities, against powers, against the rulers of the darkness of this world, against spiritual wickedness in high places. Wherefore take unto you the whole armour of God, that ye may be able to withstand in the evil day, and having done all, to stand. Stand therefore, having your loins girt about with truth, and having on the breastplate of righteousness; and your feet shod with the preparation of the Gospel of peace; above all, taking the shield of faith, wherewith ye shall be able to quench all the fiery darts of the wicked. And take the helmet of salvation, and the sword of the Spirit, which is the Word of God" (Eph. 6:10-17).

Enter the battle with this armament. You will go home the victor because Christ has fought and conquered for you. He will fight and conquer in you and set the crown of glory on you.

Man doesnt live on bread alone but on every word that God speaks.
Matthew 4:4

15th century Temptation of Christ

31. Will I Fall Away?

The afflicted person says: How many soldiers of Christ were surrounded by the devil's deceit and returned from battle not as the conquerors but as the conquered? How many made a good beginning but later lost God's grace and everlasting life? I am afraid of God's hidden counsel. When I consider God's secret decrees, terror grabs me in body and soul.

The comforter says: You are right to fear and tremble (Phil. 2:12), recognizing the weakness of your flesh and the power of the devil. You are right to consider the example of those who have fallen from salvation. But guard against the idea that the cause of this falling away is some unconditional divine decree of damnation.

God has not unconditionally decreed to give up some believers and to let them go astray. "For the gifts and calling of God are without repentance" (Rom. 11:29). Former believers who have lost salvation are lost by their own fault, not because of some unconditional decree of damnation. They turned themselves away from God by their own free will.

The Savior, the Spirit, faith, grace, and everlasting life are always closely connected. As long as a regenerate person remains in faith, he remains in Christ. Whoever remains in Christ remains in God's grace, and the Holy Spirit dwells in him. Where the Holy Spirit is, there follows the fruits of the Spirit. Those who sin maliciously against their conscience drive away the Holy Spirit, give up faith, and reject everlasting life.

By the power of the Spirit you should be certain of perseverance and salvation, but not in such a way that you fall into carnal security. The infallible promises of God free you from doubt. The admonitions and threats of God make free from carnal security. In this life there is security only in God's promises. In this life full of temptation, everyone who thinks he is standing must take heed that he does not fall (1 Cor. 10:12).

Look with one eye of your heart at God's mercy, but with the other at God's justice. From faith in God's mercy let there be in your heart a confident hope for perseverance. But from fear of

God's justice let there be a terror of carnal security. "The Lord taketh pleasure in them that fear Him, in those that hope in His mercy" (Ps. 147:11). Our inward man should hope and trust, but the outward man should fear and tremble.

32. Am I Written in the Book of Life?

The afflicted person says: Only they persevere who are written in the book of life. How can I know that I am written in it?

The comforter says: The book of life is Christ. It is called "the book of life of the Lamb" (Rev. 13:8; 21:27). Being written into this book is nothing other than the election of the believers to everlasting life, which takes place in Christ. For it is said of the believers that they have been chosen in Christ before the foundation of the world (Eph. 1:4) and that their names were written in the book of life from the beginning of the world (Rev. 17:8).

As with election so with being written in the book of life; one may not judge in advance but only afterwards. As many as have been ordained to life, hear the Word of salvation, believe in Christ, show the fruit of the Spirit, and persevere in the faith. "He that believeth on the Son of God hath the witness [of God] in himself" (1 John 5:10). The Holy Spirit bears witness in the hearts of believers that they are God's children (Rom. 8:16) and are written in the book of life. Those whom God has chosen from eternity, whose names are written in heaven (Luke 10:20), He calls through the Word and justifies through faith in Christ (Rom. 8:29-30). Such faith is shown in calling on God, being patient under the cross, and desiring sanctification.

A wholesome consideration of election and the book of life must begin with the wounds of the Crucified. Whoever believes in Him and perseveres in faith has been justified and is written in the book of the living (Rom. 10:9). Or have you not been accepted into God's grace through Baptism? Have you not been cleansed from sins by the blood of Christ? Have you not been renewed by the Holy Spirit? Those are clear signs that you have been written in the book of life. Believers "are all the children of God by faith in Christ Jesus. For as many of you as have been baptized into Christ have put on Christ" (Gal. 3:26-27).

God has written not some tables of fate but rather a book of life. He has chosen us in Christ before the foundation of the world.

Seek your election and your writing in the book of life in Christ alone.

Beyond All Reasonable Doubt

He is Risen!

Sketch after the 1632 painting of Hendrick Terbruggher

33. Fear of Death

The afflicted person says: It is good for me to cling to Christ. I do not want to let Him out of my heart. I want to persevere in true faith in Christ so that I will some day reign with Him. But I am still not free from all fear of death and still do not sense such strength of the Holy Spirit that I would, with the apostle, have a fervent desire to depart (Phil. 1:23).

The comforter says: It is a weakness of our flesh that we yearn more eagerly for this passing life than for the future, lasting life. From that comes the fear and horror of death. But to overcome this fear by the Spirit's power and grow in strength in the inward man, consider these heavenly truths. Even the hairs of our head are all numbered (Matt. 10:30). "The number of his months are with Thee, Thou hast appointed his bounds that he cannot pass" (Job 14:5). All our days were written in His book before any of them existed (Ps. 139:16). You should be satisfied with His fatherly will.

By grace God has given you life. He has wondrously drawn you from your mother's womb. He has guarded and protected you from a thousand dangers. If He takes back the soul which He gave you, He is not taking away what is yours but what is His. One has no complaint against him who asks back a possession that has been lent.

God translates the soul that He takes from you into the joys of the heavenly paradise, adorns it with great glory and precious gifts, and will some day restore it in that condition to the body. The body, which is put to bed in the grave, shall later become a more glorious and more precious dwelling place of your soul. "It is sown in corruption; it is raised in incorruption : it is sown in dishonor; it is raised in glory: it is sown in weakness; it is raised in power: it is sown a natural body; it is raised a spiritual body" (1 Cor. 15:42-44).

Your soul has been created by the Father, redeemed by the Son, and indwelt by the Holy Spirit. Commend it humbly and joyfully into God's faithful hands and say with David (Ps. 31:5), Stephen (Acts 7:59), and Christ (Luke 23:46): "Into Thine hand I commit my spirit: Thou hast redeemed me, O LORD, God of truth" (Ps. 31:5).

You may be comforted, even in the throes of death, with the presence and help of God. You hold in faith to Christ as your Mediator. You know that by His death He has taken away the power of your death and by His resurrection has again brought you righteousness and everlasting life. You are justified by faith. You have peace with God. When dying, you will be lifted up by the Father in heaven so that you say with Job, "Though He slay me, yet will I trust in Him" (Job 13:15).

The Lord says, "I will be with him in trouble; I will deliver him, and honour him. With long life will I satisfy him, and shew him My salvation" (Ps. 91:15-16). Neither death nor life nor any other creature can separate you from the love of God (Rom. 8:38-39). You are in Christ Jesus, Who is an eternal King and our Savior to eternity.

Death has such a terrifying appearance because the Law accuses us, because sin is so ugly, and because the thought of everlasting damnation attacks us. For "the sting of death is sin; and the strength of sin is the Law" (1 Cor. 15:56). Think fervently on the comfort which is given us in advance against these horrors, and the horrifying outward form of death will disappear and turn into the form of the most restful sleep of all.

34. The Wages of Sin

The afflicted person says: Death has come into the world by sin, and death is the well-deserved wages of sin. How should I not be afraid of death?

The comforter says: In and of itself death is the wages of sin and a punishment from God's anger. But for those who believe in Christ it has become the sweetest sleep. Those who have been born again and believe in Christ still carry in their flesh the remnants of sin (so that the body is subject to death because of sin dwelling in it). But the Spirit of life is there because of righteousness (Rom. 8:10). They are justified from their sins through faith in Christ. The sin that still remains in their flesh is not reckoned to them but is covered by God's grace.

The life of the believer's soul does not end in death. The Holy Spirit, the Spirit of truth, describes the death of the pious with sweet names. What the unwise see as "dying," the Holy Spirit calls "being gathered to his people" (Gen. 25:8; 35:29; 49:33), into the communion of the church triumphant in heaven with those who have gone before in faith.

Death is not an end but a change; not a banishment but a migration; not an annihilation but a blessed transfer of the soul. The soul is called home to peace. It is not destroyed but moves up to true life. Through death believers move from the sinful life to a life free from sin and come to peace and rest (Is. 57:2). They come from constant strife to a haven of peace; from the stormy sea to the calm harbor; from worldly labor to heavenly rest. They depart to be with Christ, which is far better (Phil. 1:23). They are led from the temporary dwelling of this life to the heavenly fatherland, from vexation with the ungodly to blessed communion with Christ in heaven.

As draft animals are unharnessed after work; as chains are removed from prisoners; so believers are unharnessed by death from the painful yoke of this weary world, freed from the darkness of this vale of tears, and carried to a better life (see Heb. 11:5). In death, believers emigrate from the land of pilgrimage to be at home with the Lord in the heavenly palace (2 Cor. 5:1-8).

He should fear death who has no desire to go to Christ. He can have no desire to go to Christ who does not believe that he will reign with Christ. They rest from their labors (Rev. 14:13); for not the person but only the misery of the believer ends in death. If this life is laborious, its end is an alleviation. So death is something good. Through death and burial believers are sown (1 Cor. 15:38ff.) on the field of the Lord. For the bodies of the godly shall afterwards, like the most precious grains of wheat, flourish into life again.

There speak little seeds in the bosom of earth
Of earthen, clay bodies with immortal worth.
For outwardly be they so dead and so dry,
Yet send they forth new greening shoots ne'er to die.

The land must be plowed, and the field must be sown
When in it at last the seed corn is thrown.
It looks very small and to all must appear
Most powerless, impotent, barren, and sere.

But see how it moves as from some secret sources,
And how it arises with increasing forces!
It breaks out and upward with power and strength.
In stillness were formed for it pathways at length.

So also the bodies which here now we have
Will someday be buried, for each its own grave.
But for them remains when this world is no more
An honor, a life, and a glory in store.

For first it descends in the horror of death.
The crown and the life only then come to faith.
And then is there life in the unending light.
In God's holy, gracious, and merciful sight.
                    Stigelius, a Wittenberg poet

The bones of believers will flourish like grass (Is. 66:14) when the spring of everlasting life breaks in.

They fall asleep and lie in soft slumber (2 Sam. 7:12; Is. 26:20; Dan. 12:2; Matt. 9:24; John 11:11; 1 Cor. 15:6; 1 Thess. 4:13). As we in sleep rest from work and recover from weariness, so we are brought through death from all labor and pain to rest and gather new strength of soul and body so that we more willingly and more fully accomplish the work for which we were created and for which we have been redeemed by Christ — while the soul in heaven lives and rejoices.

In sleep we do not worry about what goes on around us and are not disturbed. Those who have died with faith in Christ rest without worry or anxiety and no longer know the misery of this life. As we wake from sleep, so death will not be everlasting. The hour will come when we hear the voice of Christ, Who calls us from the grave to go forth to new life (John 5:28-29). Augustine said, no one can wake the sleeper from his bed as easily as Christ can wake the dead from the graves.

From all that it is clear that the apostle is correct in calling the believers' death a gain (Phil. 1:21). It is gain to escape sin. It is gain to get out of the way of something worse. It is gain to arrive at something better. "Precious in the sight of the Lord is the death of His saints" (Ps. 116:15). For them it is good because of rest, better yet because of security, best of all because of salvation.

35. The Pains of Death

The afflicted person says: I am not afraid of death but only of the pains of death. I have watched as the eyes of dying persons broke open, as their ears became deaf, as their tongues became stiff. I have seen the sweat and anxiety of death, the shuddering and weakness of death. I have heard the groaning and sighing of the soul that has to leave its house, the body.

The comforter says: All who believe in Christ are guarded against the pains of death or the pains are at least lightened for them. Christ took upon Himself the most bitter aspect of death: the sense of God's anger. So let us throw the wood of the cross (see Ex. 15:25), on which Christ died for us, into our death, and it will become a gentle sleep for us.

Christ says, "Verily, verily, I say unto you, If a man keep My saying, he shall never see death" (John 8:51). He will not see everlasting death and will also not experience the horrifying form of temporal death. Even if we taste a little bitterness from the cup of death, it is insignificant compared to the stream from which Christ drank for our sakes (Ps. 110:7). What is this little sip compared to the whole cup (Matt. 26:42) which the Father gave Christ to drink completely in our place?

Our death is like a cleansing medicine for soul and body. Through it the poison of sin is driven out of our flesh. What if a bit of bitter herb is mixed with the purifying drink? Our death is a midwife for everlasting life. What if there is some pain as the baby that is born also bears some of the pains of birth? No birth takes place without pain. The pain will be brief, but the day of our death will be a birthday to everlasting life.

Narrow is the gate that leads us to life. What if we come in for a bit of pressure in going through? Christ is our Leader and the One Who breaks the path for us (Mic. 2:13). We should cling to Him in faith so that we go with Him through the gate of death and find the way to everlasting life, which He knows well (Ps. 16:10).

Sin still dwells in our flesh. What if the flesh feels some

fear of death because of the remnants of sin? Our conscience has peace in Christ, Who made peace with God by His death and gives us peace by His resurrection (Rom. 5:1; Eph. 2:14ff.). Death retains no sting with which it could wound our soul. With its fangs it grabs our heel; but Christ has taken away its poison. It can never inject any into us.

36. An Early Death

The afflicted person says: I am being called out of this life too early. God is taking me away in the midst of my days (Ps. 102:24). I am afraid that is a sign of God's anger because "bloody and deceitful men shall not live out half their days" (Ps. 55:23).

The comforter says: Nothing that has ripened is ripe too soon for God. Long life is a gift of God; but a short life is not always a sign of His wrath. God often lets His believers leave this world relatively early so that they are free of the danger of sin, enter the safety of heaven, and need not experience plagues which are more troublesome than death.

"Come, My people, enter thou into thy chambers, and shut thy doors about thee: hide thyself as it were for a little moment, until the indignation be overpast" (Is. 26:20). "The righteous perisheth, and no man layeth it to heart: and merciful men are taken away, none considering that the righteous is taken away from the evil to come. He shall enter into peace: they shall rest in their beds, each one walking in his uprightness" (Is. 57:1-2).

The tree remaining fruitless, bare,
That never greens nor blossoms fair, I
s axe's prey. No good comes out.
So one removes the worthless sprout,
But no one harms the fruitful tree.
It stands its ground for all to see.
But Christians, though they fruitful be,
Are often sooner yet set free.

The believer always dies best, whether he dies in age or in youth. Is it all that sad for you to be freed sooner from this vale of tears? The sooner the Prince of the army calls you away from your post in this life, the sooner He brings you to the place of rest, peace, and victory.

37. I Could Do More for God's Kingdom

The afflicted person says: I could continue to serve the Lord's church, as much as I am able, if God would only let me live longer for that purpose.

The comforter says: You must leave it to God's will and wisdom how long He leaves you active in the service of His church on earth. So just say with the excellent teacher, Ambrose of Milan, "I have not lived in such a way that I would have to be ashamed to live longer among you; but I am also not afraid of dying, for we have a gracious Lord indeed."

If God has equipped you with the ability to teach for the blessing of His church, He knows how to equip others in the same way. If you, like the apostle, do not know which of the two to prefer; if you have the desire to depart and to be with Christ, which would be far better, or to remain in the flesh for the benefit of the church; then you know that dying is your gain, but living is a benefit to the church (Phil. 1:23).

None of us lives to himself, and none of us dies to himself. If we live, we live to the Lord (so that we can win yet more souls for Him). If we die, we die to the Lord (so that we follow Him when He calls us from our post by His gracious will). Whether we live or die, we belong to the gracious and almighty Lord from Whom neither life nor death can separate us (Rom. 14:7-8; 8:38-39). You have listened to the will of the Lord so that you might faithfully serve His church. Listen to Him and gladly accept His will when He calls you to the church triumphant.

It is good that out of love you are concerned for the growth of the church. But in faith you must leave the direction and preservation of the church to the Lord. In this matter there is nothing as good and truly pious as when one gives himself wholly and completely to the will of God and commends the exclusive power over life and death to Him in confident prayer.

As Bernard of Clairvaux said, the Lord will give us either what we ask or something better. "Commit thy way unto the LORD; trust also in Him; and He shall bring it to pass" (Ps. 37:5).

Peter & John Race to the Empty Tomb

Drawing after painting by
Eugene Burnand

38. Have I Shortened My Own Life?

The afflicted person says: I fear that I have shortened my life by my sins. If so, how could I hope for God's presence and help in death? No better life after death awaits one who is at fault for his own death.

The comforter says: That is true in the case of those who commit suicide, which is against God's will. Do not even think of forming such a godless plan. No one has the right to kill himself. Instead of escaping the trouble of this world, he would fall into everlasting trouble. It would not make sense to do so because of past sins. This life is needed for repentance. No one may do it out of desire for a better life after death. He who is guilty of his own death can expect no better life after death.

If your soul is plagued by the thought that you have shortened your life by immoderate eating or drinking or any other kind of excess; then repent for that, trust Christ's merit, and intend to lead a better life. God has promised forgiveness of all sins to those who repent, and He will be gracious to you.

King Manasseh was a bloodthirsty man, but when he repented, he still reached the glory of everlasting life (2 Chron. 33). The thief on the cross was receiving the due reward of his deeds (Luke 23:41), but when he believed in Christ, he entered paradise with the Savior. Our first parents brought death upon themselves and their descendants. Yet they were lifted up by the life-giving promise of Him Who should tread on the snake (Gen. 3:15). If you have followed these people in their sins, follow them also in repentance.

The hand of the Lord has not been shortened, and His mercy has not been weakened by the length of the years. The door of mercy has not yet been closed as long as we are still given time for repentance.

39. Love for Life

The afflicted person says: I would like to enjoy this life and its pleasure longer. I would like to live longer under the blessings which God has given me in this life.

The comforter says: We should not have a perverted love for this life greater than our love for God. We owe the Lord a heart full of love. We love God too little if we love anything else that we do not love for God's sake. Our hearts should be emptied of that perverted love and filled with the love of God instead.

Does this life give us such great joy even though it is dangerous and difficult? What is living long other than suffering long and sinning long? If the walls in our house were shaking and the roof were trembling, if the rotten house threatened us with imminent collapse, would we not move out right away? If we were on a ship and a great storm made shipwreck inevitable, would we not head for port? The world is shaking and sinking and testifying to its fall in that things grow old and come to an end. Why do we not thank God for the blessing of being taken away from the collapse, shipwreck, and threatening blows?

As winds rouse the sea so that it threatens people in ships, so the onslaughts of the godless stir up the world to confuse the hearts of believers. So confusingly does the enemy pursue his work that one does not know what one should flee first. If the government is not against us, Satan stirs up the hearts of individuals, even our own family members. He knows how to cause discord between brothers so that the house is shaken at all four comers and begins to collapse. Then Christians should flee from it. Christians should be eager to depart in peace.

This life outwardly resembles a precious nut, but when it is opened with the knife of truth, there is nothing inside. If there is anything good in this life, the good is incomparably better in that life. This one consists in faith; that one consists in sight. We sojourn here; we abide there. We labor here; we rest there. This life is a road; that one is a homeland.

Here we fight the enemy; there we reign without enemies.

Here we face opposition; there we face none. Here we curb fleshly lusts; there we have only spiritual delights. Here we are concerned about victory; there we are secure in victorious peace.

Here we need help in temptations; there we rejoice without temptation. Here we forgive the guilt of others and need forgiveness for our sins; there we suffer nothing more that we need to forgive and do nothing more for which we need to be forgiven. Here we have unhappiness; there we have only blessedness. Here we see good and evil; there we see only good.

Which life should we prefer? Let go of the wrongful desire for this fleeting life and do not lose the inheritance of everlasting life. Possess the things of this world in such a way that you are not possessed by them. Let your possessions stand under the control of your heart so that the heart is not conquered by the love of earthly things. Why are you not concerned for that which is better? The heavenly follows the earthly; the greater follows the lesser; the eternal follows the worthless.

> All Scripture is inspired by God & is useful for teaching, showing what is wrong, improving & training in right living so that a man of God is ready & equipped for every good work.

40. Separation from Spouse, Children, and Family

The afflicted person says: I must leave my dear wife and children, my friends and relatives. Who will care for my family? Who will protect and comfort them?

The comforter says: God is a Father for the fatherless and a Judge for the widows (Ps. 68:5). Commend them to His Care and protection. Your God will be the God of your seed after you (Gen. 17:7). They are not only yours but also God's children, and more God's children than yours, for He has invested more in them. You need not doubt His fatherly care for them. David testifies: "I have been young, and now am old; yet have I not seen the righteous forsaken, nor his seed begging bread" (Ps. 37:25). God promised heavenly treasures for His children and will not let them die of hunger. He gave them life; He will not deny them what they need for life.

Do not be so concerned about your family that you forget your soul. Christ says, "If any man come to me, and hate not his father, and mother, and wife, and children, and brethren, and sisters, yea, and his own life also, he cannot be My disciple" (Luke 14:26). He explains that in another place: "He that loveth father or mother more than Me is not worthy of Me: and he that loveth son or daughter more than Me is not worthy of Me" (Matt. 10:37). The Lord is calling you away through death. Do not love wife and child so much that you hesitate to follow God's call with a joyful heart. Put love for God before love for children; love for your Bridegroom Christ before love for your spouse. One should not love the gift more than he loves the Giver.

You are losing dear ones now; you will find them again dearer still. We all have to leave this life. Dear ones who have departed are not lost to us but have merely preceded us. According to God's promise, in that life they will be dearer to us as we know them better. Then we will love and be loved without any danger of discord.

If your relatives are dear to you, your Brother Christ is

dearer yet. If it was sweet to be close to your relatives, it will be sweeter yet to come "unto Mount Sion, and unto the city of the living God, the heavenly Jerusalem, and to an innumerable company of angels, to the general assembly and church of the firstborn, which are written in heaven, and to God the Judge of all, and to the spirits of just men made perfect" (Heb. 12:22-23).

41. Deafness in Dying

The afflicted person says: If my ears become deaf when I am dying, will my heart be left without comfort and be made anxious by Satan's terror?

The comforter says: Do not forget the comfort of the Holy Spirit, Who "beareth witness with our spirit, that we are the children of God" (Rom. 8:16). The Spirit lifts our spirits up when we face anxiety of heart in the struggle of death. He is the true and highest Comforter (John 15:26). If sight is dimmed, the Holy Spirit will give you the true light; if hearing is lost, He will bring you the life-giving comfort of the soul through His Word that is already known and remembered in your heart.

Where human comfort stops, God's comfort starts. Look at the martyrs! They were ready to face the most horrible tortures. To them the rack was a rose; ashes were jewels; iron chains were golden crowns; manacles were bracelets; and threatening swords flashed with the shining rays of heavenly light. Who did that in their hearts, Who comforted them in their pains? The Holy Spirit! His comfort is stronger than the whole world, stronger than the accusations of the devil.

Do you think that the Holy Spirit would lift up our hearts through our whole life but not during the struggle with death? Do you think that, when this body dies, the dwelling place of the Holy Spirit is destroyed? Christ lives in you (Gal. 2:20). He dwells in your heart through faith (Eph. 3:17). His lips are gracious (Ps. 45:2), and the sweet aroma of his grace will make your heart glad even when earthly senses disappear. His Word, which you have often heard, will echo in your heart even if your ears are totally deaf. "The Spirit of the Lord GOD is upon Me; because the Lord hath anointed Me to preach good tidings unto the meek; He hath sent Me to bind up the brokenhearted, to proclaim liberty to the captives, and the opening of the prison to them that are bound" (Is. 61:1; Luke 4:18). "The Lord GOD hath given Me the tongue of the learned, that I should know how to speak a word in season to him that is weary" (Is. 50:4).

Hold on to Christ with firm trust of the heart. Commend

yourself to Him in the prayer of faith. He will comfort you at the right time. He will lift up your stricken heart with the Word of the Gospel. He will bind up your fatally wounded heart. He will proclaim freedom to your heart when you are led captive by death. He will proclaim an opening of prison when you are thrown into the dungeon of death.

42. Why Do the Redeemed Still Die?

The afflicted person says: If Christ has redeemed us from death, why do I still have to die? If Christ has overcome death, why does death still claim victory?

The comforter says: Christ saved His people from their sins (Matt. 1:21), not so that sin would no longer dwell in the flesh (in this life we remain sinful), but so that He would not have to damn believers forever. He redeemed us from death, not so that we would no longer be subject to temporal death (our body is mortal because of sin, Rom. 8:10), but so that we would be free from everlasting death.

The death of the soul is the real death. Christ has redeemed us from that by taking the anguish of hell upon His own soul. Jesus made even temporal death sweet for us; a death in name but in truth a sleep; the end of death and the beginning of true life (1 Cor. 15:24). True believers die daily because of the tribulations of this life. Their death is an end to tribulation. Through the gates of death they enter a quiet and everlasting life. Their death is the beginning of everlasting life.

Christ's death is a plague to our death (Hos. 13:14). This plague has not yet totally killed our death (it pricks our heels with its thorns), but the heart has taken the antidote to death. The power of this plague will finally kill death itself. Death is the last enemy. Christ will completely destroy it on the last day (1 Cor. 15:26). This strong, armed man will be overcome by a stronger One (Luke 11:22) Who will forcibly take away his spoils.

Death must be seen with spiritual eyes. Its fury is void and powerless. It has been conquered and captured by Christ. It wants to deprive believers of their lives, but it leads them to true life. It tries to kill soul, but the soul is unharmed. It wounds only the body, which will one day also be torn from the jaws of death. It wants to bring believers to eternal death, but it leads them to eternal life.

43. Fear of the Dust

The afflicted person says: I will be buried in the earth and turn into dust. "I have made my bed in the darkness. I have said to corruption, Thou art my father: to the worm, Thou art my mother, and my sister" (Job 17:13-14).

The comforter says: Do not look at the dust to which your body will return. Look at the future resurrection from the dust. If with Job you have called corruption your father, with Job say also: "I know that my Redeemer liveth, and that He shall stand at the latter day upon the earth: and though after my skin worms destroy this body, yet in my flesh shall I see God" (Job 19:25-26).

The blessed resurrection of our bodies is proven by the words of Scripture, important reasons, and the example of those who have risen.

Many Bible passages in both the Old and the New Testaments speak very clearly about the resurrection. The blood of Abel cries to the Lord from the ground (Gen. 4:10). In God's eyes, he still lives. In death the patriarchs were gathered to their people (Gen. 25:8; 35:29; 49:33) and are still the people of the living God. God is "the God of Abraham, the God of Isaac, and the God of Jacob" (Ex. 3:6), and "God is not the God of the dead, but of the living" (Matt. 22:32). Abraham, Isaac, and Jacob live before God in their spirits, and their bodies will some day be called back to life.

Job says, "I know that my Redeemer liveth, and He shall later awaken me from the earth" (Job 19:25, [Luther's translation]). Isaiah says: "Thy dead men shall live, together with My dead body shall they arise. Awake and sing, ye that dwell in dust: for thy dew is as the dew of herbs, and the earth shall cast out the dead" (Is. 26:19). "Your bones shall flourish like an herb" (Is. 66:14). The Lord says to the dry bones: "I will cause breath to enter into you, and ye shall live: and I will lay sinews upon you, and will bring up flesh upon you, and cover you with skin, and put breath in you, and ye shall live; and ye shall know that I am the LORD" (Ezek. 37:5-6). Daniel says: "Many of them that sleep in the dust of the earth shall awake, some to everlasting life, and some to shame and everlasting contempt" (Dan. 12:2).

The One Who is the Truth (John 14:6) says: "The hour is coming, in the which all that are in the graves shall hear His voice, and shall come forth" (John 5:28-29). "This is the Father's will Which hath sent Me, that of all which He hath given Me I should lose nothing, but should raise it up again at the last day. And this is the will of Him That sent Me, that every one which seeth the Son, and believeth on Him, may have everlasting life: and I will raise him up at the last day" (John 6:39-40; see vv. 44, 54). "I am the resurrection, and the life: he that believeth in Me, though he were dead, yet shall he live: and whosoever liveth and believeth in Me shall never die" (John 11:25-26).

Paul expresses the "hope toward God... that there shall be a resurrection of the dead" (Acts 24:15). "For this corruptible must put on incorruption, and this mortal must put on immortality.... Then shall be brought to pass the saying that is written, Death is swallowed up in victory" (1 Cor. 15:53-54). We know "that He Which raised up the Lord Jesus shall raise up us also by Jesus, and shall present us with you" (2 Cor. 4:14). "For our conversation is in heaven; from whence also we look for the Saviour, the Lord Jesus Christ: Who shall change our vile body, that it may be fashioned like unto His glorious body, according to the working whereby He is able even to subdue all things unto Himself" (Phil. 3:20-21). "For if we believe that Jesus died and rose again, even so them also which sleep in Jesus will God bring with Him" (1 Thess. 4:14). John "saw the dead, small and great, stand before God;.... And the sea gave up the dead which were in it" (Rev. 20:12-13).

In addition to these clear words of Scripture, there are all kinds of reasons and firm supports. The apostle draws this conclusion: if Christ is risen, we will also rise. Christ's resurrection is the key to our graves. Christ has "become the firstfruits of them that slept" (1 Cor. 15:20). Just as according to God's ordinance, the harvest followed the offering of the firstfruits (Ex. 23:19; Lev. 23:20), the harvest of the general resurrection follows the firstfruit of Christ's resurrection.

Christ is our Head. What happens first to the Head, happens

later to the members. So the apostle proclaims with all confidence: God "hath raised us up together [with Christ], and made us sit together in heavenly places in Christ Jesus" (Eph. 2:6). For our flesh and blood is in the Man Christ. Where He reigns, we will reign. Where our blood has dominion, we will have dominion. Where our flesh stands in glory, we will have glory.

As death came through one man, the first Adam, so the resurrection came through one Man, the second Adam. As we die in Adam, we are made alive in Christ (1 Cor. 15:21-22). Adam's fall had the power to bring us death; should Christ's resurrection not have the power to gain for us the resurrection of life?

By His glorious resurrection Christ showed Himself to be the Conqueror of all His enemies, even death, which He will finally completely destroy. Christ is an eternal King. He will raise the citizens of His kingdom from death so that they live with Him forever. Christ has freed not only our soul but also our body from the yoke of sin and ordained both for everlasting life. The body will have to arise from the dust so that it can enter into the possession of the life which Christ has gained for it.

From all of that it becomes clearly evident that Christ is the Guarantor of our resurrection.

Further our bodies are temples of the Holy Spirit (1 Cor. 3:16). The Spirit will not permit His temples to remain in dust but will rebuild them and make them much more glorious than they were in this life.

Our bodies are sanctified by the body and blood of Christ in the holy Supper. How could they possibly remain in the grave? How can the flesh that is nourished with the body and blood of the Lord decay and never attain life? As the bread that is taken from the earth is, by the Word of Christ, no longer common bread but a meal of both earthly and heavenly elements, so our bodies, which receive the holy Supper, have the hope of the resurrection.

Finally there are the examples of those who have been raised, who were called to life again by Christ by His own power, or through the prophets and apostles by Christ's power. As advance messengers of everlasting life, they give us, who are one with them in faith and confession, a testimony to the future resurrection.

44. The Resurrection Is Contrary to Reason

The afflicted person says: Belief in the resurrection of the body is contrary to human reason. In my heart I hope for the resurrection, but that hope is weakened by disturbing thoughts.

The comforter says: The basis of our faith is God's Word, not human reason. We are to take every thought captive to this obedience to Christ (2 Cor. 10:5). God "is able to do exceeding abundantly above all that we ask or think" (Eph. 3:20). So think about God Who promises it and will do it. God's words are not only words but also deeds. God can do things that we cannot understand. The power of God Who speaks is proof enough of the deed. For Him Whose flesh could not be destroyed, it will be easy to grant that this corruptible put on incorruption (1 Cor. 15:53).

Many images of the future resurrection are presented to us in creation. "That which thou sowest is not quickened, except it die: and that which thou sowest, thou sowest not that body that shall be, but bare grain, it may chance of wheat, or of some other grain: but God giveth it a body as it hath pleased Him, and to every seed his own body" (1 Cor. 15:36-38). He Who gives life to the dead seed, which nourishes you in this life, can do much more, even raise you to live forever.

The light which perishes daily shines forth again. The darkness goes and comes. Starlight dies and lives again. The seasons end and start again. Fruits are devoured and come again. Only when it dies and disintegrates does the seed rise again ever more fruitfully.

Everything is preserved in decline, and from decline everything is rebuilt. The day dies and is always buried in darkness. Yet the light comes to life again with all its glory and blessing. It breaks out of its grave, the darkness. It rules until the night, which also has its glory, comes to life again. The moon, which had disappeared with the month, becomes full again. Winter and summer and spring and fall come again with their powers, characteristics, and fruits.

The earth stands under heavenly cultivation. It clothes the trees after they had lost their leaves. It paints the flowers anew. It plants herb and grass anew. It turns from robber into preserver. It takes so that it may give again. It destroys so that it may protect. It empties so that it may fill. It decreases so that it may increase. It presents everything more fully and more gloriously than before.

Every condition returns. What is called loss is gain. All this order of things returning is a testimony to the resurrection of the dead. God recorded it in His works before His writings. He preached through His power before His words. He gave you nature as a teacher. He sent prophecy later so that as a student of nature you would more easily believe the prophecy; so that you would believe when you hear what you have already seen everywhere; so that you would not doubt that God will raise the body since you already know that He renews all things. Are such pictures in nature superfluous? Is God weaker than nature?

See in yourself a testimony to the resurrection. If God created everything, including your body, He can also raise the body, no matter its state of decay. He Who has made something can certainly make it anew. It takes more to make something than to remake it. It takes more to make a beginning than to make a new beginning. So believe that it is easier to raise and restore the body than it was to create it.

"... and you will call Him Jesus, because He will save His people from their sins."
Luke 1:21

45. Purgatory

The afflicted person says: I fear that I will be punished in purgatory. I am oppressed by many kinds of sinful weakness. God may enter into judgment with me (Ps. 143:2) and condemn me to purgatory.

The comforter says: Anyone with whom God enters into judgment, anyone who has not been reconciled to God during this life, is condemned by God not to some purgatory, where he would be tormented for a limited time, but to hellfire, where he will burn forever. But anyone who repents for his sins and believes in Christ has the assurance and promise of his Savior that after death he need fear no place of pain and torment. For the Lord says: "Verily, verily, I say unto you, He that heareth My Word, and believeth on Him That sent Me, hath everlasting life, and shall not come into condemnation; but is passed from death unto life" (John 5:24).

The Word of truth knows only two types of people: penitent and impenitent, believers and unbelievers; and only two places after death: that of comfort and that of torment, heaven and hell. We find nothing in Scripture about any third type of person or any third place. There are only two places: the eternal kingdom and the eternal fire. There is no third place. One can only be with the devil if he is not with Christ.

Christ says: "He that believeth and is baptized shall be saved; but he that believeth not shall be damned" (Mark 16:16). "He that believeth on Him is not condemned: but he that believeth not is condemned already, because he hath not believed in the name of the only begotten Son of God" (John 3:18). John the Baptist says: "He that believeth on the Son hath everlasting life: and he that believeth not the Son shall not see life; but the wrath of God abideth on him" (John 3:36). The righteous shall go into everlasting life, but the damned shall go into everlasting punishment (Matt. 25:34, 41, 46).

This division of the godly from the godless does not take place first on the last day but immediately after death. That is taught by the example of the rich man whose soul was thrown into hell and of the pious Lazarus whose soul the angels carried into paradise (Luke 16:22-23). It is taught by the example of the converted thief to whom Christ promised entrance into heaven on the same day on which he had to die (Luke 23:43). It is taught by the Spirit of truth: "Blessed are the dead which die in the Lord from henceforth" (Rev. 14:13). There is no other payment or propitiation for our sins than that in the blood of Christ, which cleanses us from all sin (1 John 1:7). "The punishment lies on Him so that we may have peace" (Is. 53:5 [Luther's translation]).

Anyone who believes in Jesus Christ is righteous and has peace with God (Rom. 5:1). He has passed from death to life (1 John 3:14). No torment will touch him after death.

"Let Us Preach Only Christ & the Catechism"
Luther 1532

46. The Strictness of the Last Judgment

The afflicted person says: I fear the strictness and the terror of the Last Judgment. Above the strict Judge; below the open hell; inside the nagging conscience; outside the burning fire; to the right sins that condemn me; to the left devils that frighten me. Satan will accuse me. My sins will accuse me. My conscience will accuse me.

> *Oh, how many an anxious thought*
> *Which the Judge's look has brought!*
> *That reveals my every sin.*
> *It is known what I have been.*
> *Bernard of Clairvaux.*

No one can escape God's power, elude His wisdom, divert His justice, or avoid His judgment.

The comforter says: If you believe in the Son, you will not be condemned (John 3:18) by His judgment. If you hear the Word of Christ and believe in Him, you will not come into judgment (John 5:24). Your case will not be handled by His severe court since He has delivered all His believers from the wrath to come (1 Thess. 1:10). Judgment Day will be terrifying only for unbelievers because of the punishment. It will be sweet for believers because of the crown. For the former it is a day of wrath and judgment. For the latter it is a day of grace and boundless reward. "Lift up your heads," says the Son of God, "for your redemption draweth nigh" (Luke 21:28).

A bride is not afraid of the arrival of her bridegroom. Through faith your soul is betrothed to Christ. When He appears on Judgment Day, He is coming to lead you, as His bride, to the heavenly wedding (Rev. 19:7). Is that something to fear?

That will be a day of liberation. It will make us completely and perfectly Christ's servants. It will deliver us from every evil trouble. It will bring us completely out of the constant struggle with the flesh and out of all spiritual danger. It is a day of refreshing

(Acts 3:19), for it brings those who are faint and thirsty out of the heat of tribulation to a place of rest and to the fountain of living waters. Let every believer in Christ say: "Even so, come, Lord Jesus!" (Rev. 22:20).

If we love Christ, we will be eager for His coming. It would be backwards to be afraid of the arrival of Him Whom one loves; to pray, Thy kingdom come, and yet to be afraid that such prayer may be heard.

Where does this fear come from? Because He comes as Judge? Do you think He will be unjust, angry, or unfavorable to you? Do you have to be afraid that your Attorney, your Advocate, will conduct your case poorly? Nothing of the sort! Think Who is coming! Why are you not rejoicing? For Who is coming to judge you other than the One Who already came to be judged in your place?

Do not be afraid of the accuser, of whom Christ has already said, "Now shall the prince of this world be cast out" (John 12:31). Do not fear that your Attorney will conduct your case poorly. For your Advocate, your Defender is the One Who will be your Judge. He will represent you and your case. He will testify for you. You have no reason at all to fear the coming Judge.

Your Judge will be your Attorney, your Advocate (1 John 2:1-2). Your Judge has promised His saints that they will judge the world. Your Judge is He in Whom you have been chosen from eternity for life. Your Judge is also your King; how could a king destroy his people? Your Judge is He Whose true member you have become through faith; how could a head destroy its members? "Who shall lay anything to the charge of God's elect? It is God that justifieth. Who is he that condemneth? It is Christ That died, yea rather, That is risen again, Who is even at the right hand of God, Who also maketh intercession for us" (Rom. 8:33-34).

How can He let them be lost whom He has taken under His protection, for whose sake He came into the world, so that they would not be lost? The believers have not despised the Gospel but have believed it. Christ's voice called them to conversion: "Come unto me, all ye that labour and are heavy laden, and I will give you rest" (Matt. 11:28). His voice will call them to take possession of the kingdom of heaven: "Come, ye blessed of My Father, inherit the kingdom prepared for you from the foundation of the world" (Matt. 25:34). The Judge is He from Whose countenance grace and truth proceed (John 1:17). Grace has blotted out the sins of the believers; truth has given them the promise of everlasting life.

You need not be afraid in any way, not even of the terrible passing away of heaven and earth. "Heaven and earth shall pass away: but My words shall not pass away" (Luke 21:33). "The Word of our God shall stand for ever" (Is. 40:8). You trust this Word; you will also remain forever. Your treasure is not the wealth of this world but joy and bliss in the kingdom of heaven. Let the world burn up; it is enough for you that Christ lives and protects you. Heaven and earth will pass away and be gone, but you have the promise of a new heaven and a new earth. "I create new heavens and a new earth [wherein dwelleth righteousness, 2 Pet. 3:13]: and the former shall not be remembered" (Is. 65:17: see Rev. 21:1). The inn of your pilgrimage may collapse. You have the everlasting dwelling place in the heavenly homeland.

You need not even fear any more the accusations of Satan, the Law, and your sins. Your sins have been thrown into the depths of the sea (Mic. 7:19), into the abyss of divine mercy. God has cast all your sins behind His back (Is. 38:17) that they shall not be mentioned (Ezek. 18:22). Satan will not bring them up from the sea and will not dare to place them before the Judge's face. Your sins are forgiven, covered (Ps. 32:1), blotted out (Ps. 51:1). They will not be brought before the court (Is. 43:25; Jer. 31:34). The accusation which the devil attempts against believers will be in vain. He will be confronted by the fact that the handwriting that was against you has been blotted out by Christ's blood (Col. 2:14). It will be in vain if sin accuses you. Christ has forgiven you. It will be in vain if the Law accuses you. Christ has kept the Law and appeased God's anger against your sin.

You need not even fear that Christ will come suddenly for judgment. The day of the Lord will come "as a thief in the night" (1 Thess. 5:2), but "God hath not appointed us to wrath, but to obtain salvation by our Lord Jesus Christ" (v. 9). Judgment Day is no object of fear for those for whom the kingdom was prepared and who have been chosen in Christ, both "before the foundation of the world" (Matt. 25:34; Eph. 1:4). Commend the care of your soul into the faithful hands of God. He will preserve it in death and judgment, reunite it with the body, and lead it to everlasting glory in the heavenly place of joy. Amen.

www.ingramcontent.com/pod-product-compliance
Lightning Source LLC
Chambersburg PA
CBHW072101290426
44110CB00014B/1772